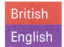

Personal Best

B1 Pre-intermediate

Student's Book and **Workbook** combined edition **B**

Series Editor
Jim Scrivener

Student's Book Authors
Bess Bradfield with
Graham Fruen

Workbook Authors
Elizabeth Walter
and **Kate Woodford**

STUDENT'S BOOK CONTENTS

		LANGUAGE			SKILLS	
		GRAMMAR	PRONUNCIATION	VOCABULARY		
7	**City living**	▪ present perfect with *just*, *yet* and *already* ▪ present perfect with *for* and *since*	▪ *just* and *yet* ▪ *for* and *since*	▪ city features ▪ transport	**LISTENING** ▪ a video looking at commuting around the world ▪ listening for facts and figures ▪ final /t/ sound	**WRITING** ▪ writing an essay ▪ giving opinions **PERSONAL BEST** ▪ an opinion essay about a problem
7A	Life in the city — p58					
7B	The daily commute — p60					
7C	A life in three cities — p62					
7D	I think it's a great idea — p64					
8	**Food for thought**	▪ *too*, *too many*, *too much* and *(not) enough* ▪ *must(n't)* and *(not) have to*	▪ *too much sugar* ▪ sentence stress	▪ food and drink ▪ adjectives to describe food	**READING** ▪ an article about a course run by a Gelateria in Bologna ▪ scanning for specific information ▪ linkers to contrast information (*although*, *but*, *however*)	**SPEAKING** ▪ sounding polite ▪ making and responding to invitations **PERSONAL BEST** ▪ arranging to go out with a friend
8A	Sweet but dangerous — p66					
8B	Ice-cream university — p68					
8C	You must eat your vegetables — p70					
8D	First dates — p72					
7 and **8**	REVIEW and PRACTICE — p74					
9	**Money and shopping**	▪ *used to* ▪ the passive (present and past simple)	▪ *used to/use to* ▪ sentence stress	▪ money verbs ▪ shopping	**LISTENING** ▪ a video about the importance of shopping centres ▪ identifying attitude and opinion ▪ filler expressions	**WRITING** ▪ writing a formal email ▪ noun forms of verbs **PERSONAL BEST** ▪ an email complaining about a purchase
9A	He used to be poor — p76					
9B	What a bargain! — p78					
9C	Going, going, gone! — p80					
9D	I'd like a refund — p82					
10	**Sport and fitness**	▪ past perfect ▪ reported speech	▪ *'d* and *hadn't* ▪ weak form of *that*	▪ sports and competitions ▪ parts of the body	**READING** ▪ an article about wheelchair rugby ▪ finding information in a text ▪ giving examples	**SPEAKING** ▪ being helpful ▪ making enquiries **PERSONAL BEST** ▪ asking for information about a service or product
10A	Winning is everything — p84					
10B	Rock 'n' roll on wheels — p86					
10C	He said it had changed his life — p88					
10D	Could you tell me …? — p90					
9 and **10**	REVIEW and PRACTICE — p92					
11	**At home**	▪ *-ing*/infinitive verb patterns ▪ articles (*a/an*, *the*, no article)	▪ sentence stress ▪ *the*	▪ household objects ▪ housework ▪ words to describe materials and clothes	**LISTENING** ▪ A video about what we really think of housework ▪ understanding and interpreting information ▪ omission of words	**WRITING** ▪ making writing interesting ▪ adjective order **PERSONAL BEST** ▪ writing an interesting description of a house
11A	Dream home — p94					
11B	The truth about housework — p96					
11C	Technology you can wear — p98					
11D	House swap — p100					
12	**People and relationships**	▪ defining relative clauses ▪ uses of the *-ing* form and the infinitive with *to*	▪ sentence stress ▪ word stress	▪ relationships ▪ relationship verbs	**READING** ▪ an infographic showing how much time we spend on different activities ▪ interpreting data ▪ expressing approximate quantities	**SPEAKING** ▪ responding modestly ▪ giving thanks **PERSONAL BEST** ▪ thanking someone for a favour
12A	Bring your parents to work — p102					
12B	In our lifetime — p104					
12C	Long-distance love — p106					
12D	Thanks a million! — p108					
11 and **12**	REVIEW and PRACTICE — p110					

Grammar practice **p124**   Vocabulary practice **p148**   Communication practice **p162**   Irregular verbs **p175**

Language App, unit-by-unit grammar and vocabulary games

WORKBOOK CONTENTS

		LANGUAGE			SKILLS	
		GRAMMAR	PRONUNCIATION	VOCABULARY		
7 City Living		■ present perfect with *just, yet* and *already* ■ present perfect with *for* and *since*	■ *just* and *yet* ■ *for* and *since*	■ city features ■ transport	LISTENING ■ listening for facts and figures	WRITING ■ writing an essay
7A	p38					
7B	p39					
7C	p40					
7D	p41					
7 — REVIEW and PRACTICE	p42					
8 Food for thought		■ *too, too many, too much* and *(not) enough* ■ *must(n't)* and *(not) have to*	■ *too much sugar* ■ sentence stress	■ food and drink ■ adjectives to describe food	READING ■ scanning for specific information	SPEAKING ■ making and responding to invitations
8A	p44					
8B	p45					
8C	p46					
8D	p47					
8 — REVIEW and PRACTICE	p48					
9 Money and shopping		■ *used to* ■ the passive	■ *used to/use to* ■ sentence stress	■ money verbs ■ shopping	LISTENING ■ identifying attitude and opinion	WRITING ■ writing a formal email
9A	p50					
9B	p51					
9C	p52					
9D	p53					
9 — REVIEW and PRACTICE	p54					
10 Sport and fitness		■ past perfect ■ reported speech	■ *'d* and *hadn't* ■ weak form of *that*	■ sports and competitions ■ parts of the body	READING ■ finding information in a text	SPEAKING ■ making enquiries
10A	p56					
10B	p57					
10C	p58					
10D	p59					
10 — REVIEW and PRACTICE	p60					
11 At home		■ *-ing*/infinitive verb patterns ■ articles	■ sentence stress ■ *the*	■ household objects ■ housework ■ words to describe materials and clothes	LISTENING ■ understanding and interpreting information	WRITING ■ making writing interesting
11A	p62					
11B	p63					
11C	p64					
11D	p65					
11 — REVIEW and PRACTICE	p66					
12 People and relationships		■ defining relative clauses ■ uses of the *-ing* form and the infinitive with *to*	■ sentence stress ■ word stress	■ relationships ■ relationship verbs	READING ■ interpreting data	SPEAKING ■ giving thanks
12A	p68					
12B	p69					
12C	p70					
12D	p71					
12 — REVIEW and PRACTICE	p72					

Writing practice **p77**

UNIT 7 City living

LANGUAGE present perfect with *just*, *yet* and *already* ■ city features

7A Life in the city

1 Discuss the questions in pairs.
 1 Do you live in a city, a town or a village?
 2 Do you like where you live?
 3 What are the good and bad things about it?

2 **A** Look at the picture. Which city is it?

B Match the words in the box with the parts of the city.

> pavement   traffic lights   bridge
> bike lane   pedestrian crossing   bench

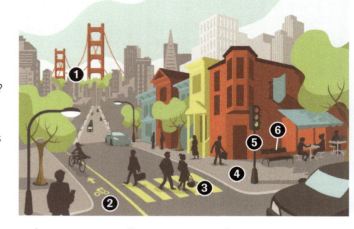

1 _____ 2 _____ 3 _____ 4 _____ 5 _____ 6 _____

Go to Vocabulary practice: city features, page 148

3 **A** Read the text. Who is more positive about the city: Alex or Megan? _____

B Read the text again and match the headings in the box with the paragraphs.

> Cost of living   Job opportunities   The weather   The people   Transport   Entertainment

Big City

San Francisco is one of the fastest growing cities in the USA. Today, we speak to two people who recently moved here and find out their first impressions of living in the city.

Alex, 25, is an IT professional and has just moved to San Francisco from London.

1 _____
There are so many tech companies here; it's really exciting. I've joined a networking group to meet people from the industry and I've already been to a couple of events. Have I found a job yet? No … but I'm sure I will soon! At least I have my visa!

2 _____
In my apartment block, there are people of all nationalities, as well as from other places in the USA. I haven't met all my neighbours yet, but I love living in a city where everyone is different.

3 _____
Whatever you're interested in, there's always something going on. I've already been to the theatre twice and seen a baseball game, and I only arrived two weeks ago!

Megan, 27, has moved to San Francisco from her hometown in Idaho to study Engineering.

4 _____
San Francisco is expensive and you need a good salary to live here. I've rented a room in a shared house, but after I've paid the rent, it doesn't leave me with much money for other things.

5 _____
All my friends told me that the summers wouldn't be as good as back home. It hasn't been too cold yet, but it can get really foggy, especially when you're near the ocean.

6 _____
The traffic here is terrible, so forget driving! Public transport can get really crowded, too, so I've just bought myself a bike. It's one of the best ways to get around the city, and the bike lanes are great.

58

present perfect with *just*, *yet* and *already* ■ city features   **LANGUAGE**   **7A**

4 **A** Who said sentences 1–4: Alex or Megan?
1 I've _____ bought myself a bike.
2 Have I found a job _____ ?
3 It hasn't been too cold _____ .
4 I've _____ been to the theatre twice.

B Complete the sentences with the words in the box. Check your answers in the text.

already   just   yet (x2)

5 Answer the questions about the sentences in exercise 4. Then read the Grammar box.
1 Which tense is used in the sentences? _____
2 Which word do we add in questions and negative sentences to talk about something we expected to happen before now? _____
3 Which word do we add to sentences to talk about something that happened earlier than we expected? _____
4 Which word do we add to sentences to talk about something that happened very recently? _____

Grammar   present perfect with *just*, *yet* and *already*

Something that happened very recently: *I've just seen* Peter in the street.
Something that happened earlier than we expected: *He's already* finished his homework.
Something we expected to happen before now: *Have* you had lunch *yet*? *I haven't seen* the film *yet*.

Go to Grammar practice: present perfect with *just*, *yet* and *already*, page 124

6 **A** ▶ 7.3 **Pronunciation:** *just* and *yet* Listen and repeat the words. Pay attention to the /j/ sound (*yet*) and the /dʒ/ sound (*just*).
1 /j/   **y**et   **y**oung   **y**ou   **u**sually
2 /dʒ/   **j**ust   **j**ob   **g**ym   bri**dge**

B ▶ 7.4 How do you say the sentences? Listen, check and repeat.
1 Have **y**ou joined a club **y**et?
2 She's **j**ust **u**sed the machine.
3 I already have a **j**ob.
4 An**g**ela hasn't arrived yet

Go to Communication practice: Student A page 162, Student B page 170

7 ▶ 7.5 Complete the phone conversation between Alex and his friend Josh. Use the present perfect form of the verbs in the box and *just*, *yet* and *already*. Listen and check.

find   have (x2)   make   meet   not see

Josh Hi Alex, it's Josh here. How's it going in San Francisco?
Alex Great, thanks. I'm really enjoying it.
Josh Have you ⁱ _____ any friends ² _____ ?
Alex Yes, I ³ _____ quite a few people. Actually, I ⁴ _____ lunch with two guys who work for an internet company.
Josh Great! And ⁵ _____ you _____ a job ⁶ _____ ?
Alex No, not ⁷ _____ . But I ⁸ _____ three interviews. I'm waiting to hear back from them.
Josh Well, good luck! Oh, what's the Golden Gate Park like?
Alex I ⁹ _____ it ¹⁰ _____ ! I'm too busy ... but I might go this weekend.

Josh

8 **A** Make a list of things you have already done and things you still have to do this week.

B In pairs, ask and answer the question *Have you ... yet?* about your partner's list. Give more information in your answers.

A Have you been to the supermarket yet?
B Not yet. I'm going shopping tonight, though.
A Have you called your parents yet?
B Yes, I've already called them twice this week.

Things to do
– go to the supermarket
– call my parents
– meet up with my friends

Personal Best   Write about the town or city you live in.   59

7 SKILLS LISTENING listening for facts and figures ■ final /t/ sound ■ transport

7B The daily commute

1 Is traffic a problem in your town/city? How do most people travel to work?

2 Look at the pictures in exercise 4. In pairs, use the words in the box to describe them.

> traffic jam   drive   rush hour   commuter   passenger   car park
> platform   take the train   parking space   public transport

In picture a, people are driving to work, but there's a really bad traffic jam.

Go to Vocabulary practice: transport, page 148

3 ▶ 7.8 Look at exercise 4. Which cities do pictures a–c show? Watch or listen to the first part of *Learning Curve* and check.

a _____   b _____   c _____

Skill   listening for facts and figures

We often have to listen for specific information.
- Before you listen, focus what type of information you need to listen for. For example, is it a number, a person, a time, a place, etc?
- Listen for 'clues'. For example, if the information is an age, you might hear 'old' or 'years'.
- Write the exact word(s) you hear. Then read the sentences to make sure they make sense.

4 A Read the Skill box. Match the types of information in the box with the gaps in the text.

> a specific time   a verb (x2)   a noun   an adjective (x2)   a period of time (x2)   a number (x2)

B ▶ 7.8 Watch or listen again and complete the text with the correct words.

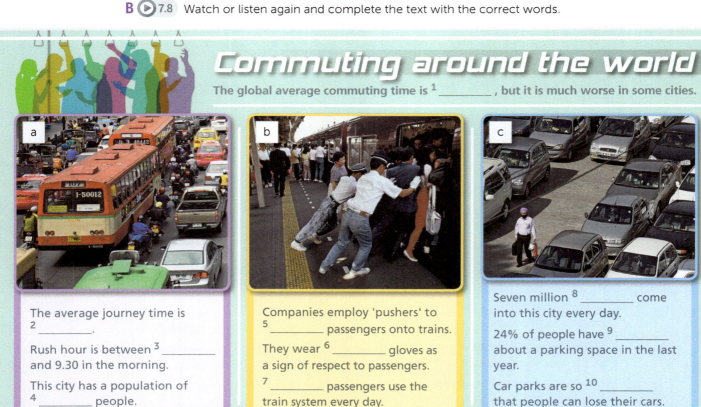

Commuting around the world

The global average commuting time is ^{1}_____, but it is much worse in some cities.

The average journey time is ^{2}_____.

Rush hour is between ^{3}_____ and 9.30 in the morning.

This city has a population of ^{4}_____ people.

Companies employ 'pushers' to ^{5}_____ passengers onto trains.

They wear ^{6}_____ gloves as a sign of respect to passengers.

^{7}_____ passengers use the train system every day.

Seven million ^{8}_____ come into this city every day.

24% of people have ^{9}_____ about a parking space in the last year.

Car parks are so ^{10}_____ that people can lose their cars.

60

listening for facts and figures ■ final /t/ sound ■ transport   **LISTENING**   SKILLS   **7B**

5 ▶ 7.9 Watch or listen to the second part of the show. How do Mike, Sandra and Lorena get to work/university?

Mike

Sandra

Lorena

6 A Read questions 1–8. What kind of information do you need to answer them?
1 How long does Mike's journey take in total? — *a period of time*
2 What time does he usually leave his house? _____
3 What causes him problems on his commute? _____
4 Which city is Sandra in? _____
5 How often does she usually travel with Bonnie? _____
6 How far is it to Sandra's work? _____
7 How long does it take Lorena to walk to university? _____
8 How much does she spend on public transport? _____

B ▶ 7.9 Watch or listen again. Answer the questions.

7 Discuss the questions in pairs.
1 How do you get to work/university/class?
2 How long does it take you?
3 What time do you set off?
4 Do you ever have any problems?
5 Who do you travel with?
6 How does the journey make you feel?

8 ▶ 7.10 Listen to the sentences from the show. When are the /t/ sounds in **bold** pronounced?
1 What time do you se**t** off?
2 My bigges**t** problem is pedestrians.
3 I'm here in fron**t** of our building in New York.
4 Today, I'm jus**t** listening to my car radio.

Listening builder final /t/ sound

English speakers don't often pronounce the /t/ sound at the end of a word when the next word begins with a consonant. If the next word begins with a vowel sound, they link the sounds together.
I get ͜ off the train.   *I ge(t) to chat with my good friend.*
There's still a lot ͜ of traffic.   *She doesn'(t) drive.*

9 ▶ 7.11 Read the Listening builder. Listen and complete the sentences.
1 The _____ _____ to get to work is to drive, _____ _____ is impossible.
2 I _____ _____ at 8.00 and _____ _____ me over an hour.
3 The traffic _____ _____ completely, so we _____ _____ and walked.
4 It's the _____ _____ in the world for commuting, but they _____ _____ buy a car.
5 I _____ _____ taking the metro. I feel _____ _____ _____ people come out of the station.

10 A In pairs, prepare a talk of 1–2 minutes about the transport system in your city or country. Use the ideas in the boxes.

| the type of transport people use | the cost and frequency of public transport | the problems commuters have | suggestions for people visiting your city or country |

B Work with another pair. Take it in turns to listen, then ask at least one question.

Personal Best Write a paragraph about the advantages and disadvantages of one type of transport.

7 LANGUAGE present perfect with *for* and *since*

7C A life in three cities

1 A Look at the pictures. Try and answer the questions in pairs.
1 Who is the person?
2 What is her job?
3 Which film has she been in?
4 What nationality is she?

B Read the introduction in the text and check your answers.

A TALE OF THREE CITIES

She won an Oscar for her first film, *12 Years a Slave*, in 2013. Since then, the Kenyan actress Lupita Nyong'o has become a Hollywood superstar and appeared on red carpets and magazine covers all over the world. We look at the three cities which have shaped this talented actress.

MEXICO CITY
Lupita was born in 1983 in Mexico City, where her father was working at a university. The family returned to Kenya when she was just a few months old, but at the age of 16, Lupita went back to Mexico for a year to learn Spanish. She's spoken Spanish since 1999, and has even given TV interviews in Spanish.

NAIROBI
Lupita went to school in Nairobi, and this is where she first started acting. Her first big performance was at the age of 14 when she played Juliet in *Romeo and Juliet*. One of her happiest memories is of climbing the mango trees in her grandmother's village and eating the fruit straight from the branches!

NEW YORK
Lupita has lived in Brooklyn, New York, since 2013, and this is now her home. When she isn't working, she spends her time doing yoga and cooking her favourite dishes like *enchiladas verdes*. She also loves travelling into Manhattan on the subway to go shopping, just like anyone else in New York! The big question is: Where next for Lupita?

2 Read the rest of the text. Are the sentences true (T) or false (F)?
1 Lupita has been very famous since 2013. ____
2 She has had an interest in acting for over ten years. ____
3 She has spoken Spanish since she was a small child in Mexico. ____
4 She has lived in New York for most of her life. ____

3 Look at sentences 1–4 in exercise 2. Choose the correct options to answer the questions. Then read the Grammar box.
1 Are the situations in the sentences finished? *yes / no*
2 Which tense are the verbs in? *present continuous / present perfect*
3 When do we use the word *since*? *for a point in time / for a period of time*
4 When do we use the word *for*? *for a point in time / for a period of time*

Grammar — present perfect with *for* and *since*

For situations that started in the past and continue in the present:
I've **worked** as an actress **for** twenty years.   She **hasn't seen** me **since** 2010.

Look! We use **for** for a period of time and **since** for a point in time:
I've had this car **for** six months.   I've had this car **since** February.

Go to Grammar practice: present perfect with *for* and *since*, page 125 present perfect with *for* and *since*   **LANGUAGE 7C**

4 A ▶ 7.13   **Pronunciation:** *for* and *since* Listen and repeat the sentences. Pay attention to the rhythm. Are *for* and *since* stressed or unstressed words?

1 She's lived in New York since 2013.
2 She hasn't been to Mexico for a few years.

B ▶ 7.14   Underline the stressed words in the sentences. In pairs, practise saying them. Listen, check and repeat.

1 I've lived in this house for six years.
2 She's known him since 1995.
3 I haven't seen him for months.
4 They've had the car since March.

Go to Communication practice: Student A page 162, Student B page 170

5 ▶ 7.15   Listen to the conversation and answer the questions.
1 Where do you think the people are?
2 How do Laura and Pete know each other?
3 What is Jess's job?
4 What do Laura and Jess discuss at the end?
5 Do you think connections are important to find a good job?

6 A Complete the questions with the past simple or present perfect form of the verbs in brackets.
1 Where _____ Laura and Pete _____? (meet)
2 How long _____ Jess _____ in LA? (be)
3 How long _____ Jess _____ in Toronto? (live)
4 How long _____ Jess _____ scripts for TV and films? (write)
5 What _____ she _____ before she was a writer? (do)
6 How long _____ Laura and Pete _____ the idea for the TV comedy series? (have)

B ▶ 7.15   Listen to the conversation again. Ask and answer questions 1–6 in pairs.

7 A Complete the circles with information about you.

- the name of an important friend
- the name of your street
- your occupation (job/student, etc.)
- a hobby you enjoy
- an important possession
- a place you want to visit
- something you use every day
- something you are frightened of

B In pairs, ask and answer the question *How long have you ...?* with a suitable verb and the information in the circles. Try to give more information.

A *How long have you known Martin?*
B *I've known him since we were at secondary school together. We were in the same class.*
A *How long have you had your phone?*
B *I've had it for six months. It was a birthday present from my brother.*

Personal Best   Think of someone you know well and write a paragraph about his/her life. Try and use the present perfect with *for* and *since*.

7 SKILLS WRITING writing an essay ■ giving opinions

7D I think it's a great idea

1 Look at the pictures in exercise 2. Discuss the questions in pairs.
1 How often do you use your mobile phone each day?
2 Do you call people when you are in the street? If so, who?
3 Do you use your phone on public transport? If so, what for?
4 Do you send messages when you go out with friends? If so, how often?
5 Do you think we use our phones too much? Why/Why not?

2 **A** Read the title of the essay. What does the verb *ban* mean?
   a make something illegal ☐   b make something easier ☐
  B Read the essay. Does Kai agree or disagree with the question?

Is it time to ban smartphones in public?
Kai Meng

Smartphones are amazing inventions and help us in lots of different ways, but I'm worried that we use them too much. Every day, I see hundreds of people using their phones in the city and it's causing some serious problems.

Firstly, I believe smartphones can be dangerous. When people are walking in the street and sending messages at the same time, or if they're listening to music with headphones, they don't concentrate on the traffic and it's much easier for them to have an accident.

The second reason is that I think speaking on phones in public is annoying. If you're on a train or in a restaurant, you don't want to hear someone else's conversation. In my opinion, people should wait to call their friends and colleagues in private unless it's a real emergency.

Finally, banning smartphones in public is a good idea because it would make people more sociable and talk more. Even when some people meet up with their friends, they spend half the time checking their phones and going on social media. If they didn't have their phones, they'd talk to each other more and they'd have a much better time.

In conclusion, although there are lots of advantages of smartphones, I think we should ban them in public. Personally, I think this would be safer for pedestrians, nicer for passengers on public transport and would help us to communicate with each other more.

3 Answer the questions about the essay. Then read the Skill box.
1 How many reasons for banning smartphones does Kai give? What are they? Which paragraphs are they in?
2 What is the purpose of paragraph 1? *to introduce the topic / to summarize all his reasons*
3 What is the purpose of the final paragraph? *to introduce the topic / to summarize all his reasons*

> 🔧 **Skill**   writing an essay
>
> In essays, we discuss a topic and give our point of view.
> - Organize your ideas into paragraphs (introduction, reasons and conclusion).
> - Explain the reasons for your opinions in separate paragraphs. Give examples or evidence to support them.
> - Use sequencers, like *firstly*, *the second reason*, *finally* and *in conclusion* to help readers.

writing an essay ■ giving opinions   **WRITING**   SKILLS   **7D**

4 Look at the pictures. In pairs, think of some reasons why we *shouldn't* ban smartphones in public.

5 A Match the halves to make sentences. Did you have similar ideas?

1 We can check emails, read documents
2 I believe this is very important
3 Personally, I love being able to watch
4 In my opinion, smartphones
5 They make our lives safer, more
6 Secondly, smartphones make
7 In conclusion, I don't think we should
8 The first reason is that phones help us
9 The last reason is that they are
10 Modern technology has changed

a the way we communicate.
b have made our lives better in three different ways.
c stay in touch with each other.
d for our safety.
e us work more efficiently.
f and organize meetings outside the office.
g lots of fun and keep us entertained.
h films or play games when I'm on the train.
i ban smartphones in public.
j efficient and even more fun.

B Which sentences come from:
the introduction? _____   paragraph 3? _____   the conclusion? _____
paragraph 2? _____   paragraph 4? _____

6 A In pairs, use the sentences in 5A to help you write an essay against banning smartphones in public.

B Which essay is more convincing: Kai's or the one you wrote in exercise 6A? Do you think we should or shouldn't ban smartphones in public?

7 Read the essay in exercise 2 again. Underline any phrases Kai uses to give his opinion.

| Text builder | giving opinions |

We use a variety of phrases to give our opinions:
I (don't) think/believe (that) ...   *I'm worried/delighted (that) ...*   *... is a good/bad idea.*
In my opinion/view, ...   *Personally, ...*   *I would(n't) say (that) ...*

8 Read the Text builder. In pairs, give your opinions about ideas 1–5. Explain your ideas.
1 I *think / don't think* public transport should be free for everyone because …
2 Children playing computer games is a *good / bad* idea because …
3 In my opinion, learning English *is / isn't* very difficult because …
4 Personally, I *watch / don't watch* too much TV because …
5 I *would / wouldn't* say that we eat less healthily than our parents because …

9 A **PREPARE** Choose an essay title and decide if you agree or disagree with it. Give three reasons with examples and evidence to support them.

• Should universities be free for everyone?
• Do we need to ban fast-food restaurants?
• Should people who live in cities be allowed to keep pets?
• Do we need shops now that we can buy everything online?

B **PRACTISE** Write an essay giving your opinion. Use the Skill box and Text builder to help you.

C **PERSONAL BEST** Swap essays with another student and correct any mistakes. Is his/her essay convincing? How could he/she improve it?

Personal Best   Write an essay with the opposite point of view to the one in exercise 9.

65

UNIT 8

Food for thought

LANGUAGE   too, too many, too much and (not) enough   ■ food and drink

8A Sweet but dangerous

1 Put the words in the box in the correct columns. Can you add two more words to each column?

| beef | cabbage | peach | salmon | strawberry | prawns | lamb | aubergine |

fruit	vegetables	meat	fish and seafood

Go to Vocabulary practice: food and drink, page 149

2 Ask and answer the questions in pairs.
1 What did you have for breakfast?
2 What did you have for dinner last night?
3 What food do you eat if you want a snack?
4 What would you cook for a romantic dinner?
5 Are you allergic to any food?
6 Do you think you have a healthy diet? Why/Why not?

3 Look at the picture of the breakfast. Do you think it's healthy? How much added sugar do you think it contains? Read the text and check.

Most of us know that too much sugar isn't good for us. We know that we shouldn't eat lots of chocolate or drink too many fizzy drinks. But how much do we really know about the other food we eat?

Australian film-maker, Damon Gameau, decided to investigate the 'hidden' sugar in food. He spent 60 days only eating products advertised as 'healthy', such as low-fat yoghurt, cereal bars, fruit juices and sports drinks. But instead of feeling healthier, Damon gained 8kg in weight and started to have health problems. The reason? The high levels of sugar that manufacturers add to many food products to make them taste better. The breakfast pictured here looks good, but the juice, cereal and yoghurt actually contain fourteen teaspoons of extra sugar!

Damon says that food companies are not honest enough about the amount of sugar that they add to products; their marketing makes us believe we're eating and drinking healthily, when really, we are not. The World Health Organization recommends a daily limit of 25g (about six teaspoons) of sugar. That means there's enough sugar in three quarters of a can of cola for one day.
After Damon's experiment finished, he returned to his usual diet of fresh fruit, vegetables, meat and fish. His weight went down and his health problems disappeared. He still enjoys a little chocolate from time to time, but he finds that most processed food now tastes too sweet.
So next time you're in the supermarket, remember to check how much sugar is in that packet of 'healthy' cereal before you buy it!

4 Tick (✔) the best title for the article. Explain your answer.
1 Is sugar good or bad for you? ☐
2 How to lose weight in 60 days ☐
3 The truth about sugar and processed food ☐
4 Five unhealthy foods to avoid ☐

5 Discuss the questions in pairs.
1 Did the text surprise you? Why/Why not?
2 Do you think people in your country eat too much sugar?
3 How often do you check how much sugar is in the products you buy?
4 Should the government do anything about sugar in food? If so, what?

too, too many, too much and *(not) enough* ■ food and drink | **LANGUAGE** | **8A**

6 A Complete the sentences with the words in the box. Check your answers in the text.

> too   too much   too many   not   enough

1 We shouldn't drink _____ fizzy drinks.
2 _____ sugar isn't good for us.
3 Food companies are _____ honest enough.
4 There's _____ sugar in three quarters of a can of cola for one day.
5 Most processed food tastes _____ sweet.

B Match the words from sentences 1–5 with the definitions. Then read the Grammar box.

1 *too / too much / too many*
2 *enough*
3 *not enough*

a less than necessary
b more than necessary
c the right amount

📖 **Grammar** *too, too many, too much* and *(not) enough*

More than necessary:
*It's **too** noisy. I can't concentrate.*
*You put **too much** milk in my coffee!*
*There are **too many** people on the bus.*

The right amount:
*We have **enough** eggs to make a cake.*
*Is the room warm **enough** for you?*

Less than necessary:
*I don't have **enough** time.*
*The car isn't fast **enough**.*

Personal Best

Go to Grammar practice: *too, too many, too much* and *(not) enough*, page 125

7 A ▶8.3 **Pronunciation:** *too much sugar* Listen and repeat the sentence from the text. Pay attention to the sounds in **bold**: /uː/, /ʌ/ and /ʊ/.

Too m**u**ch s**u**gar isn't good for us.

B ▶8.4 How do you say the words? Listen, check and repeat.

c**oo**k s**ou**p c**u**p f**oo**d en**ou**gh p**u**t bl**oo**d sh**ou**ld **u**se

8 ▶8.5 How do you say the questions? Listen, check and repeat. Ask and answer the questions in pairs.

1 Do you have enough time to cook dinner every night?
2 Do you think good food is too expensive?
3 Do you spend too much time using social media sites?
4 Do you think you have too many clothes?
5 Is your internet connection fast enough for you?
6 Do you know anyone who drinks too much coffee?

9 ▶8.6 Listen to a conversation. Tick (✔) the food that the restaurant needs to buy.

meat: lamb ☐ chicken ☐ beef ☐ turkey ☐
fish/seafood: salmon ☐ prawns ☐ tuna ☐
fruit: peaches ☐ pears ☐ coconuts ☐ strawberries ☐ pineapples ☐
vegetables: peppers ☐ lettuces ☐ cucumbers ☐ tomatoes ☐ aubergines ☐

Go to Communication practice: Student A page 162, Student B page 170

10 A Complete the sentences with your own ideas. Compare them in pairs.

1 I don't spend enough time on _____.
2 I spend too much money on _____.
3 I worry about _____ too much.
4 Sometimes, I'm too _____.
5 I have too many _____.
6 I don't think I'm _____ enough.

B Tell the rest of the class about your partner.

He doesn't spend enough time on his homework.

Personal Best Write a list of ingredients for three of your favourite dishes.

67

8 | **SKILLS** | **READING** scanning for specific information ■ linkers to contrast information

8B Ice-cream university

1 Look at the title of the article and the pictures. Discuss the questions in pairs.

1 Where do you think the university is?
2 Who do you think goes on courses here?
3 Would you like to learn how to make ice-cream?
4 What's your favourite ice-cream flavour?

> **🔧 Skill** scanning for specific information
>
> **To find a specific piece of information in a text quickly, you should scan for it.**
> - Identify the key word(s) in the question for the information you need.
> - Quickly look for the key words in the text. You can use your finger to help you.
> - Stop when you find the key word. If the information you need isn't there, continue scanning until the key word appears again.

2 Read the Skill box. Scan the text and answer the questions. The key words are <u>underlined</u>.

1 What is <u>gelato</u>?
2 When did the <u>museum</u> open?
3 How much does a <u>one-day course</u> cost?
4 When was the Gelato University <u>founded</u>?
5 What is the <u>average age</u> of students at the university?

3 <u>Underline</u> the key words in the questions. Scan the text again to answer them.

1 How many students attend the university every year?
2 What languages are lessons taught in?
3 What happens if you make *gelato* using too much sugar?
4 What is the right temperature for *gelato*?
5 How much is a visit to the museum?

4 Read the text in detail. Match the headings in the box with the paragraphs A–E.

> The secret of good *gelato*   A city to study in   If you just want a taste
> A course for everyone   A mix of students

> **◄■► Text builder** linkers to contrast information
>
> ***but:*** *There are courses that last up to five weeks,* ***but*** *I'm going to try the one-day course.*
> ***however:*** *There are courses that last up to five weeks.* ***However****, I'm going to try the one-day course.*
> ***although:*** ***Although*** *there are courses that last up to five weeks, I'm going to try the one-day course.*
> *I'm going to try the one-day course,* ***although*** *there are courses that last up to five weeks.*

5 A Read the Text builder. <u>Underline</u> examples of *but*, *however* and *although* in the text. In pairs, discuss what information is contrasted.

B Complete the sentences with *but*, *however* and *although*. Which paragraphs do they go with?

1 _____ gelato is Italian, it has an international reputation.
2 It's a complicated process, _____ after a few hours, I have a litre of pink ice-cream.
3 It's only four euros for children under thirteen. _____ , they must be accompanied by an adult.
4 I'm really looking forward to this course, _____ I've never been a 'good student'.
5 There's even a course to become a professional *gelato* taster. _____ it sounds like the dream job, I don't think I could eat ice-cream 365 days a year!

6 Discuss the questions in pairs.

1 Apart from English, are you studying anything else at the moment?
2 What courses would you like to do if you had the time and the money?
3 If you could start your own business, what would it be?

68

scanning for specific information ■ linkers to contrast information READING SKILLS 8B

A _____

The city of Bologna in Italy is home to the oldest university in the world, founded in 1088. The list of former students includes artists, politicians, poets and even film directors. However, what a lot of people don't realize is that Bologna is also home to another, much newer, university. I've signed up for a course, although I'm not going to study Law or Engineering. I'm going to learn how to make *gelato* – Italian ice-cream. Welcome to Gelato University!

B _____

The Carpigiani Gelato University was founded in 2003, and every year it attracts more than 6,000 students who want to learn how to make the perfect ice-cream. However, it isn't just about making ice-cream. Students all have the same dream of starting their own *gelato* business, so lessons include how to write a business plan, how to market your product, even how to design your own *gelateria* – or ice-cream shop. There are courses that last up to five weeks, but I'm going to try the one-day course, which costs about 100 euros.

C _____

In my class of 20, there are students from all over the world, and although my lessons are in English, there are also classes in Italian, Spanish, Chinese and other languages. The average age of the students is about 35, but company director Robert from LA is planning to move into the *gelato* business at the age of 72! 'You're never too old to try new things,' he says.

D _____

Back in the classroom, and today we're making strawberry *gelato*. However, before we start, there's a Science lesson. There's a lot of Chemistry and Mathematics, and a calculator is essential. If there's too much sugar in the mix, it won't freeze. If there isn't enough air, it will be too heavy. And it has to be served at the right temperature (5–10° C), which is much warmer than normal ice-cream.

E _____

If you're interested in *gelato*, but you haven't got the time or the money to do a course, the university also has its own Gelato Museum, opened in 2012. For five euros, you can visit the museum, discover the history of *gelato*, the technology behind it, and – of course – taste some of the different flavours! And if you're wondering how my strawberry *gelato* tasted, it was delicious!

Personal Best Write a paragraph about your school or university. Remember to use linkers to contrast information.

8 LANGUAGE *must(n't)* and *(not) have to* ■ adjectives to describe food

8C You must eat your vegetables

1 A ▶ 8.7 Look at the pictures of school lunches. Which countries do you think they are from? Listen and check.

a

b

c

B ▶ 8.7 Match the adjectives in the box with the pictures. Listen again and check.

healthy   crunchy   sweet   spicy   salty   tasty

Go to Vocabulary practice: adjectives to describe food, page 150

2 Discuss the questions in pairs.
1. Did you ever have school lunches? If so, what were they like?
2. Which dishes from your childhood did you love/hate? Why?

3 Look at the pictures. Do you recognize the man? In pairs, answer the questions. Read the text and check.
1. What is the man's job?
2. Which country is he in?
3. Why is he in this country?
4. Why does he look disappointed?

THE FOOD REVOLUTION THAT FAILED

British celebrity chef, Jamie Oliver, has tasted failure for the first time with his American TV show, *Jamie's Food Revolution.* One of the biggest health problems in the USA is obesity and Jamie thought that he could help by changing what children ate … but he found that it wasn't so easy.

In the USA, more than 32 million children eat in school cafeterias every day. Unfortunately, the meals aren't always very healthy and some children don't have to eat fruit or vegetables. Instead, many choose hamburgers and pizzas with sweet drinks like chocolate milk.

Jamie decided to change the menu at a school in Los Angeles. The cooks made different meals, including vegetarian curry, fresh salads and spicy chicken noodles. However, Jamie's experiment failed and most children threw his new recipes in the bin. With hungry children and angry parents, hamburgers and pizzas were soon back on the menu.

However, it isn't all bad news. Although Jamie's idea didn't work, things have started to change. New laws say that all schools have to serve healthier food. School meals mustn't contain too much salt, and cafeterias must offer two vegetables a day … but there's still some work to do. According to the rules, tomato sauce on pizzas counts as 'one vegetable'!

4 Discuss the questions in pairs.
1. What do you think about Jamie's experiment?
2. Why do you think it failed?
3. What would you think if he tried to change school meals in your country?

must(n't) and *(not) have to* ■ adjectives to describe food   LANGUAGE **8C**

5 A Match the halves to make sentences. Check your answers in the text.
1 Children **don't have to** a serve healthier food.
2 All schools **have to** b offer two vegetables a day.
3 School meals **mustn't** c eat fruit or vegetables.
4 Cafeterias **must** d contain too much salt.

B Answer the questions about the words in **bold** in sentences 1–4. Then read the Grammar box.
1 Which words mean 'there is a rule to do this'? _____ _____
2 Which words mean 'this isn't necessary'? _____
3 Which words mean 'this is not allowed'? _____

> **Grammar** *must(n't)* and *(not) have to*
>
> **Obligation:**
> You **must** start school at 9.00 a.m.
> Do they **have to** wear a uniform?
>
> **Prohibition:**
> Students **mustn't** use a calculator in the exam.
>
> **Not necessary:**
> You **don't have to** do the course, but you can if you want.

Go to Grammar practice: *must(n't)* and *(not) have to*, page 127

6 Choose the correct options to complete the hotel rules. Would you like to stay in this hotel? Why/Why not?

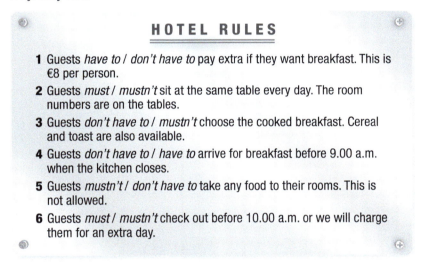

HOTEL RULES

1 Guests *have to / don't have to* pay extra if they want breakfast. This is €8 per person.
2 Guests *must / mustn't* sit at the same table every day. The room numbers are on the tables.
3 Guests *don't have to / mustn't* choose the cooked breakfast. Cereal and toast are also available.
4 Guests *don't have to / have to* arrive for breakfast before 9.00 a.m. when the kitchen closes.
5 Guests *mustn't / don't have to* take any food to their rooms. This is not allowed.
6 Guests *must / mustn't* check out before 10.00 a.m. or we will charge them for an extra day.

7 A ▶ 8.10 **Pronunciation: sentence stress** Listen to the sentences. <u>Underline</u> the stressed words.
1 People must carry an identity card at all times.
2 You don't have to buy a ticket when you get on the bus.
3 People mustn't use their mobile phones on public transport.
4 Children have to stay at school until the age of 18.
5 Parents don't have to send their children to school. They can educate them at home.
6 Everyone has to vote in national elections.

B ▶ 8.10 Say the sentences, paying attention to the stress in each one. Listen again, check and repeat.

8 In pairs, decide if the sentences in exercise 7A are true in your country.

Go to Communication practice: Student A page 163, Student B page 171

9 A In pairs, imagine you are the managing directors of a new company. Write a list of rules that will keep your employees happy and productive and make your company successful. Think about these factors:

working hours meetings food and drink social activities breaks during the day
days off / holidays working clothes communication

B Tell the rest of the class your rules.

Personal Best Write a list of rules in your place of work or university. How could you change them to make them better?

71

8 SKILLS SPEAKING making and responding to invitations ■ sounding polite

8D First dates

1 In pairs, look at the pictures of restaurants. Decide which are the best places for the situations in the box.

> business meeting   first date   meeting up with friends
> birthday celebration   lunch on your own   family meal

2 Discuss the questions in pairs.
1 How would you feel if you had a first date?
2 Where would you go on a first date?
3 Who would you ask for advice about a first date?

3 ▶ 8.11 Watch or listen to the first part of *Learning Curve*. Are the sentences true (T) or false (F)?
1 Jack feels shy about asking Eleanor out on a date. ____
2 Jack met Eleanor while he was studying at university. ____
3 He invites Simon to try his new dish and he wants his advice. ____
4 Simon thinks Jack should take Eleanor to a fish-and-chip restaurant. ____
5 Jack rings Eleanor to ask her out on a date. ____

4 ▶ 8.11 Use the words in the box to complete what Jack and Simon said. Watch or listen again and check.

> dish   great   be   in   sounds
> new   Would   that   interested
> you   trying   a   Thanks   out

Conversation builder — making and responding to invitations

Inviting:
Would you like to …?
Would you be interested in …?
Do you want to …?
Do you fancy …?
I was wondering if you'd fancy …

Accepting:
I'd love to. Thank you.
Thanks, that sounds great!
That's very kind of you.
That would be lovely.
Fantastic.

Refusing:
That's really nice of you, but I'm sorry, I can't.
I'm afraid I already have plans.
I really appreciate the invite, but …
Sorry, I think I'm busy that evening.

5 Read the Conversation builder. In pairs, take turns to invite your partner for a coffee one day this week. Refuse the first time but when he/she invites you for a coffee on a different day, accept.

making and responding to invitations ■ sounding polite **SPEAKING** SKILLS **8D**

6 **A** ▶ 8.12 Watch or listen to the second part of the show. Where do Jack and Eleanor decide to go for their date?

B ▶ 8.12 Complete the conversation with the words in the box. Watch or listen again and check.

appreciate   like   fancy   sorry   want   kind

Jack I was wondering if you'd ¹_____ having dinner with me at my restaurant?
Eleanor Oh, that's right, you're a chef. Thanks, that's very ²_____ of you.
Jack Great. I know it's short notice, but, would you ³_____ to come tonight? I have a new, special dish.
Eleanor Did you say tonight? That's really nice of you, but I'm ⁴_____, I can't. I already have plans.
Jack Well, do you ⁵_____ to go out at the weekend? Perhaps tomorrow?
Eleanor Er, I would. I really ⁶_____ the invite, but, I'm going to go visit my granddad.

7 ▶ 8.13 Listen and repeat the phrases when you hear the beeps. Do Eleanor and Jack sound polite?

Skill   sounding polite

It's important to sound polite in English, especially when you say something negative.
• Use intonation to express yourself. Flat intonation can sound rude.
• Apologize before you say something negative.
• Use longer phrases and give explanations.

8 **A** ▶ 8.14 Read the Skill box. Listen to six conversations and tick (✓) the response which sounds more polite: a or b.

1 Tom, could you help me with this box? It's really heavy.   a ☐   b ☐
2 Hi, do you fancy seeing a film tonight?   a ☐   b ☐
3 So, what did your boss think of the designs?   a ☐   b ☐
4 Would you like to get a coffee after class?   a ☐   b ☐
5 Wow! That new jacket looks great on you.   a ☐   b ☐
6 Would you be interested in seeing my band play tomorrow evening? a ☐   b ☐

B ▶ 8.15 Listen and repeat the polite responses. Explain why they are more polite.

Go to Communication practice: Student A page 163, Student B page 171

9 **A** PREPARE In pairs, look at the diagram and discuss what you could say at each stage. You can make notes.

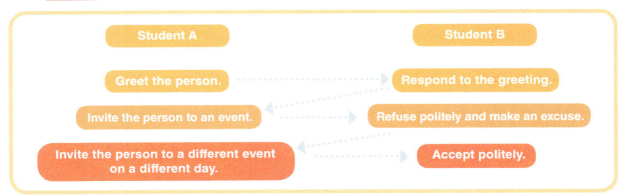

B PRACTISE Repeat your conversation until you can say it without looking at the diagram or your notes.

C PERSONAL BEST Work with another pair. Listen to their conversation. Did they use the same language as you? Was their conversation polite? In what way?

Personal Best   Write another dialogue using the diagram in exercise 9A, but use different phrases.

7 and 8 REVIEW and PRACTICE

Grammar

1 Cross (**X**) the sentence which is NOT correct.

1. a I've just called Claude.
   b I've called Claude 10 minutes ago.
   c I called Claude 10 minutes ago.
2. a I have to wear a suit at work.
   b I must wear a suit at work.
   c I haven't to wear jeans at work.
3. a I've worked here since January.
   b I've worked here for five months.
   c I've worked here since five months ago.
4. a This restaurant is too crowded.
   b This restaurant isn't quiet enough.
   c This restaurant is too much crowded.
5. a I've seen the film yet.
   b I saw the film last week.
   c I've already seen the film.
6. a You have too many clothes in the wardrobe.
   b You don't have space enough for your clothes.
   c You don't have enough space in the wardrobe.
7. a I haven't seen my parents for a month.
   b I didn't see my parents since last month.
   c I haven't seen my parents since last month.
8. a You mustn't walk on the grass.
   b You have to walk on the path.
   c You must to walk on the path.

2 Use the words in brackets to write sentences that mean the same as the first sentence.

1. It isn't necessary for Sofia to take the train.
   Sofia _____ take the train. (have)
2. I saw her five minutes ago.
   I _____ her. (just)
3. I went to the shops this morning.
   I _____ to the shops. (already)
4. We've had the car since March.
   We _____ six months. (for)
5. We need more bread.
   We _____ bread. (enough)
6. She hasn't visited me for years.
   She _____ 2012. (visited)
7. The coffee has more milk than I wanted.
   There's _____ in my coffee. (too)
8. You're not allowed to use your phone in here.
   You _____ your phone in here. (use)

3 Choose the correct options to complete the text.

Don't look down!

The city of Dubai [1]*built / has built* over 200 skyscrapers [2]*for / since* 2000 and the Burj Khalifa is the tallest of these. It's 830 m high, with 163 floors and has an incredible 24,000 windows … which all [3]*have / must* to be cleaned! The highest part of the building is [4]*too / too much* difficult for people to clean, and machines are used. However, a team of 36 men clean the rest of the building. We talk to Bibek Thapa from Nepal, who has [5]*just / yet* finished cleaning for the day.

What's the hardest part about the job?

I've climbed [6]*enough mountains / mountains enough* in Nepal not to be afraid of heights. The worst thing for me is the sun. Sometimes it's [7]*too / too much* hot and we [8]*have to / mustn't* wear protective clothes.

What's it like in bad weather?

We don't work when there's [9]*too many / too much* wind or dust because it's so dangerous.

Do you need any special equipment?

We use lots of safety equipment, obviously, but we [10]*have to / don't have to* use any special cleaning chemicals. We just use soap and water, like when you clean windows at home.

Vocabulary

1 Match the words with the definitions.

> rush hour   fresh   set off   coconut
> raw   pedestrian crossing   turkey
> give someone a lift   litter bin   commuter

1. to take someone to a place in your car _____
2. a place for rubbish when you're in the street _____
3. a person who travels to work _____
4. a large bird we can eat _____
5. a large fruit from a palm tree _____
6. to leave your house to go somewhere _____
7. food that is not cooked _____
8. a place where you can cross the road safely _____
9. the busiest time of day on the roads _____
10. food that was prepared recently _____

2 Circle the word that is different. Explain your answer.

1 passenger   platform   pedestrian   commuter
2 sour   sweet   bitter   crunchy
3 drive   ride   go by   traffic
4 beef   lamb   prawns   turkey
5 tunnel   bridge   bike lane   litter bin
6 delayed   signpost   statue   pavement
7 tuna   peach   pineapple   strawberry
8 tasty   burnt   healthy   delicious

3 Choose the correct word to complete the sentences.

1 My bus never _____ on time.
   a arrives   b gets   c drives
2 Is the fish _____? It doesn't smell very good.
   a fresh   b tasty   c healthy
3 You should _____ now or you'll be late.
   a arrive   b set off c drive
4 We're having _____ for dessert.
   a flour   b lettuce c apple pie
5 My car is in the garage, so I can't _____ to work.
   a ride   b drive   c arrive
6 A: What's on the pizza?
   B: There's tomato sauce, peppers, and _____ .
   a flour   b tuna   c cereal
7 There are no _____ on this road – it's so dark!
   a traffic lights b street lights c signposts
8 The doctor said I shouldn't eat _____ food.
   a fresh   b salty   c disgusting

4 Complete the conversations with the words in the boxes.

parking space   benches   car park
apartment block   public transport

Jo   Is your new ¹_____ near the city bridge?
Lee No, it's next to the square with the fountain and all the ²_____ to sit on.
Jo   That's a great area! Do you get a ³_____ for your car?
Lee Yes, but I use ⁴_____ to get to work because my office doesn't have a ⁵_____ .

fresh   delicious   prawns   spicy   vegetarian

Kim Don't forget you have to cook ⁶_____ food for my parents. They don't eat meat.
Jon I know. I'm going to cook a curry.
Kim Don't cook a curry! It will be too ⁷_____ for them! Why don't you cook the *paella* you made last week? It was ⁸_____! I loved it.
Jon But that had ⁹_____ in it!
Kim Oh, yeah. Can't you make it without them? Just add lots of ¹⁰_____ vegetables.

75

UNIT 9

Money and shopping

LANGUAGE   used to ■ money verbs

9A   He used to be poor

1 A Look at the title of the text and the pictures. Discuss the questions in pairs.

1 Have you ever been to a Zara shop?
2 What does Zara sell?
3 Who is the man?
4 What does the title of the text mean?

B Read the introduction and check your answers.

FROM ZERO TO ZARA

Today, he's one of the richest men in the world with a global business that is worth billions of dollars, but he used to be a poor boy from Galicia, in the north of Spain. This is the story of Amancio Ortega, the founder of the clothes company, Zara.

Amancio was born in 1936. His father was a railway worker and didn't earn much money. The family sometimes couldn't afford food and his mother used to ask for credit at the grocery store, but one day they said no. That was the moment Amancio decided to leave school and get a job. He was just 14.

Amancio's first job was in a shirt shop. He used to fold the shirts and deliver them to customers on his bike. Then he moved to another shop, where he learned a lot about the industry. Clothes used to be quite expensive and there wasn't much choice, so customers didn't use to buy many. Amancio realized that if he could produce more attractive clothes more cheaply, people would spend more money.

So, at the age of 27, and with just a little money that he'd saved, Amancio started his own business making pyjamas, which he sold to local shops. After borrowing some money from a bank, he began making other types of clothes and the business grew. In 1975, Amancio opened his first Zara shop and the company soon opened more shops in Spain.

Today, you can find Zara and the other fashion companies Amancio owns in 88 different countries around the world, but he still lives in Galicia, where he grew up.

2 Order the events from 1–8. Read the text and check.

a ☐ He worked in a shirt shop.
b ☐ Zara expanded around the world.
c ☐ He left school.
d ☐ The first Zara shop opened.
e ☐ He started to produce other types of clothes.
f ☐ Amancio was born in northern Spain.
g ☐ He used his own money to start a business.
h ☐ He asked the bank for some money.

3 What do you think Amancio Ortega is like? Why?

4 A Match the halves to make sentences. Check your answers in the text.

1 Amancio decided to
2 His mother used to
3 Customers didn't use to
4 He used to

a ask for credit.
b buy many clothes.
c leave school.
d be a poor boy from Galicia.

B Look at sentences 1–4 again and answer the questions. Then read the Grammar box.

1 Are the sentences about the past, the present or the future? _____
2 Which sentence is an action that only happened once? ____ Which tense is it? _____
3 Which sentence is a situation that was true in the past, but isn't true now? ____
4 Which sentences are actions that happened more than once in the past? ____ ____

76

used to ■ money verbs **LANGUAGE 9A**

 Grammar *used to*

Actions that happened regularly in the past, but don't happen now:
How **did** you **use to** get to school?
We **used to walk** to school. We **didn't use to take** the bus.

Situations that were true in the past, but aren't true now:
What **did** she **use to** be like?
She **used to be** quite shy. She **didn't use to be** very confident.

Look! We use the past simple for an action that only happened once.
I **went** to the shops yesterday. NOT ~~I used to go to the shops yesterday~~.

Go to Grammar practice: *used to*, page 128

5 ▶ 9.2 **Pronunciation:** *used to/use to* Listen to the sentences. How do you say the words in **bold**? Do they sound different? Listen again and repeat.

1 His family **used to** be poor.
2 He didn't **use to** earn much money.
3 Did he **use to** work from home?

Go to Communication practice: Student A page 163, Student B page 171

6 Match the words in the box with definitions 1–6. Look at the highlighted words in the text on page 76 to help you.

be worth   earn   can afford   spend   save   borrow

1 have enough money to buy something _____
2 not use money and keep it in a bank _____
3 use money to buy something _____
4 have a value of a certain amount of money _____
5 take money from someone but return it later _____
6 make money from work _____

Go to Vocabulary practice: money verbs, page 151

7 Discuss the questions in pairs.

1 What do you spend your money on?
2 Do you find it difficult to save money?
3 Do you own your home or do you rent it?
4 Which professions earn the most money?
5 Have you ever borrowed money from a bank?
6 Do you have a car? How much is it worth?
7 Do you think footballers get paid too much money?
8 Do you ever waste money on things you don't need?

8 A ▶ 9.4 Listen to five people talking about their childhood. Match the topics in the box with the speakers.

bedtime   money   toys   holidays   food

1 Rachel _____   2 Angus _____   3 Freddy _____   4 Lucy _____   5 Sam _____

B ▶ 9.4 Complete the sentences with the past simple or *used to* form of the verbs in brackets. Listen again and check.

1 The first book I _____ was *Northern Lights*. (buy)
2 Our parents _____ about us. (not worry)
3 We _____ for dinner every Sunday night. (go out)
4 My granddad always _____ me a story in bed at night. (read)
5 I _____ a Buzz Lightyear toy for my birthday one year. (get)

9 A In pairs, talk about your childhood. Use the topics in the boxes or your own ideas.

bedtime   clothes   food   holidays   money   music   school   toys and games   TV

I used to go to bed at 7.00 p.m. every night. What time did you use to go to bed?

B Tell the class some things that you found out about your partner.
He/She used to …   He/She didn't use to …

Personal Best Write ten sentences about you with the verbs from the Vocabulary practice.

77

9 SKILLS LISTENING identifying attitude and opinion ■ filler expressions ■ shopping

9B What a bargain!

1 Match the words in the box with pictures a–f.

> discount   till   shopping centre   cash   queue   receipt

Go to Vocabulary practice: shopping, page 151

2 Discuss the questions in pairs.
1 Do you prefer to shop in shopping centres, department stores, small independent shops or online? Why?
2 Have you ever found a bargain in the sales? If so, what was it?
3 Do you always try on clothes in the changing rooms before you buy them? Why/Why not?
4 How long do you keep a receipt after you have bought something? Why?
5 Do you ever go window-shopping? Why/Why not?

3 ▶ 9.7 Watch or listen to the first part of *Learning Curve*. Tick (✓) the best summary of what Ethan says.
a Shopping in the past was very different. ☐
b Shopping centres have a long history. ☐
c Shopping centres are the best place to find bargains. ☐

4 ▶ 9.7 What do sentences 1–6 refer to: *Trajan's Market* (TM), or *Grand Bazaar* (GB)? Watch or listen again and check.

1 It is over 600 years old.   ____
2 Today it's a museum.   ____
3 It has about 5,000 shops.   ____
4 It has about 250,000 visitors per day. ____
5 It's almost 2,000 years old.   ____
6 People used to live there.   ____

5 A Tick (✓) Kate's opinion of the Grand Bazaar.
a She thinks it's an interesting place for tourists. ☐
b She thinks it's a good place to go shopping. ☐
c She prefers modern shopping malls. ☐

B Can you remember what words she used to give this opinion? Read the Skill box.

Ethan

identifying attitude and opinion ■ filler expressions ■ shopping   LISTENING   SKILLS 9B

Skill identifying attitude and opinion

It's often important to understand what someone's personal opinion is.
- Listen for phrases that we use to give opinions: *I think .. , I'd say ..., to be honest ...,* etc.
- Listen for adjectives that describe feelings: *boring, excited, upset, annoyed, pleased,* etc.
- Listen for verbs that express attitude: *look forward to, prefer, love, have to,* etc.

6 ▶9.8 Watch or listen to the second part of the show. Match the reasons for going to a shopping centre in the box with the three people.

see a film   return something to a shop   meet up with friends

7 A ▶9.8 Watch or listen again. Are the sentences true (T) or false (F)?
1 Andrea is annoyed that her friends aren't coming.   ____
2 She doesn't like queues.   ____
3 Lohi is surprised at the size of the shopping centre.   ____
4 He thinks he made a mistake shopping there.   ____
5 Joan was angry because she couldn't exchange her jumper.   ____
6 She's pleased with her new jumper.   ____

B Can you remember the words and phrases that helped you to answer the questions?

8 Discuss the questions in pairs.
1 When did you last go to a shopping centre?
2 Did you buy anything? If so, how did you pay?
3 What were the last clothes you bought?
4 Did you try them on?

9 ▶9.9 Read what Andrea said. Can you understand it without the missing words? Listen and complete the sentences.

> 1_____ , I'm supposed to be meeting up with some friends, but 2_____ , they 3_____ , just texted me to say they're not coming. I'd say it's a bit rude really, but I can't do anything, so I'm just 4_____ looking around, window-shopping, 5_____ ?

Listening builder filler expressions

Fillers are words and phrases that speakers say to give themselves time to think. They don't really mean anything:
So, I bought this jacket, **like**, a week ago, **I mean**, I wanted to **kind of** return it and, **er**, get a refund. **Well**, I don't have the receipt, **you see**, because I **sort of** lost it.

10 ▶9.10 Read the Listening builder. Listen to the conversation and answer the questions.
1 What is Jason doing at the shopping centre?
2 Which filler expressions do you hear?

11 In pairs, discuss how shopping has changed from the past. Use the topics in the boxes or your own ideas.

size of shops   opening hours   location   customer service   choice   quality of products   ways to pay   prices

I think the quality of clothes used to be much better.

Personal Best Use your ideas from exercise 11 to write a paragraph about how shopping has changed.

79

9 LANGUAGE the passive

9C Going, going, gone!

1 Ask and answer the questions in pairs.
1 Have you ever been to an auction? Where was it?
2 Have you ever bought anything on an online auction website?
3 What did you buy? How much did you pay?

2 ▶ 9.11 Look at the pictures. In pairs, match four of the prices in the box with the items that were sold at auctions. Listen and check.

| $5,000 | $100,000 | $1.8m | $4.6m | $75m | $120m |

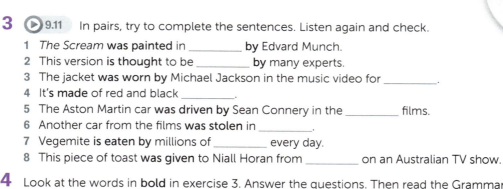

3 ▶ 9.11 In pairs, try to complete the sentences. Listen again and check.
1 *The Scream* **was painted** in _____ by Edvard Munch.
2 This version **is thought** to be _____ by many experts.
3 The jacket **was worn by** Michael Jackson in the music video for _____.
4 It's **made** of red and black _____.
5 The Aston Martin car **was driven by** Sean Connery in the _____ films.
6 Another car from the films **was stolen** in _____.
7 Vegemite **is eaten by** millions of _____ every day.
8 This piece of toast **was given** to Niall Horan from _____ on an Australian TV show.

4 Look at the words in **bold** in exercise 3. Answer the questions. Then read the Grammar box.
1 Which grammar structure is used in the sentences? _____
2 Which sentences are in the present tense? _____ Which are in the past tense? _____
3 How do we make this structure? The verb _____ + the _____ of the main verb.
4 Which word do we use before the people who do/did the action? _____
5 What is more important in the passive: the people who do/did the action or the action? _____

Grammar   the passive

Present passive
Where **are** the cars **made**?
They **are made** in Italy.
They **aren't made** anywhere else.

Past passive
When **was** the book **written**?
It **was written** in 1957.
It **wasn't published** until 2015.

Look! To say who does/did the action we use **by**.
The cars are made **by factory workers.**   The book was written **by Harper Lee.**

Go to Grammar practice: the passive, page 129

the passive   LANGUAGE 9C

5 A ▶ 9.13 **Pronunciation: sentence stress** Listen and repeat the sentence. Pay attention to the underlined stressed words.

The picture was painted in 1945.

B ▶ 9.14 Underline the stressed words. Listen, check and repeat.
1 These clothes were worn by Lady Gaga.
2 These peaches are grown in Brazil.
3 The salmon is cooked with lemon.
4 The car was driven by Lewis Hamilton.
5 These watches are made in Switzerland.
6 The bridge was opened in 2010.

Go to Communication practice: Student A page 163, Student B page 171

6 Look at the picture and the title. What do you think the text is about? How much is the box worth? Read the text and check.

FAMILY FINDS 'LOST' TREASURE AT FATHER'S HOME

This beautiful wood and gold box was made in Japan in 1640. It is one of ten boxes that were made in Kyoto by Kaomi Nagashige, a well-known Japanese artist. However, this box was thought to be lost. In fact, the Victoria and Albert Museum in London had spent over fifty years searching for it. Unknown to the museum, the box was just one kilometre away in a Kensington house. It was bought by a French engineer for £100 in 1970 and, amazingly, it was used as a table for his television! After he died, his family decided to sell it and it was identified by art experts as one of the lost Japanese boxes from 1640. It went to auction, and was sold to the Rijksmuseum in Amsterdam for £6.5 million – making the family millionaires. ■

7 A Use the words to make passive questions.
1 what / the box / make of ?
2 where / the box / make ?
3 when / the box / make ?
4 who / the box / buy / by / in 1970 ?
5 how much / the box / buy / for ?
6 what / the box / use / for ?
7 who / the box / identify / by ?
8 who / the box / sell / to / for £6.5 million?

B Ask and answer the questions in pairs.

8 Discuss the questions in pairs.
1 Do you think the box is really worth so much money?
2 How would you feel if you were the family of the French engineer?
3 What is your most important possession? Would you ever sell it?

9 Answer the quiz questions in pairs.

Quiz Time

① Where are roubles used as money?
② Who was *The Alchemist* written by?
③ When was penicillin discovered?
④ Which city in the USA is known as 'The Big Apple'?
⑤ How many Harry Potter films were made?
⑥ Which languages are spoken in Canada?

10 A In pairs, write five quiz questions with the passive form of the verbs in the boxes.

| invent | make | sing | direct | wear | write | paint | record | know | discover | use | win |

B Swap quizzes with another pair and answer the questions.

Personal Best Write about an important possession and say how much it is worth to you.

9 SKILLS WRITING writing a formal email ■ noun forms of verbs

9D I'd like a refund

1 What are the advantages and disadvantages of online shopping? Discuss the questions in pairs.
1 How often do you buy things online?
2 What do you prefer to buy in shops? Why?
3 Have you ever had a problem with something you bought online?

2 Match the problems in the box with pictures a–e.

> The wrong size was sent.   It was broken or damaged.   Part of the order was missing.
> The order arrived late / didn't arrive.   I was charged too much.

3 Read the email and answer the questions.
1 What are the three problems with Valerie's order?
2 What did she pay extra for?
3 What does she want the company to do?
4 Would you use this company?

To: info@phonetastic.com
Subject: Problems with my order (P389746-D)

Dear Sir/Madam,
I am writing to complain about the problems I have had with my online order (P389746-D).
I ordered a red X3 smartphone from your website on 14 January and I paid $4.99 extra for next-day delivery. I waited for one week, but nothing arrived, so I contacted your customer service team and I was told that it was on its way. However, the phone was only delivered yesterday – two weeks after I ordered it. Apart from the late delivery, there are two other problems with the phone. Firstly, it is the wrong colour. The phone I was sent is black – not red. And secondly, the screen is cracked. I have attached a photo so you can see what I mean. Because of these problems, I wish to return the phone and I would like a full refund, including the extra delivery charge.
I look forward to hearing from you soon.
Regards
Valerie Lemoir

---

4 A Is the style of the email formal or informal? Why?

B Order the different parts of the email. Then read the Skill box.

a ☐ say what she wants the company to do
b ☐ complain about the late delivery
c ☐ give the reason for writing
d ☐ close the email
e ☐ explain the other problems
f ☐ include a short and accurate subject line

> 🔧 **Skill** writing a formal email
>
> **We often write formal emails to people who work for other companies and organizations.**
> • Use a formal greeting: *Dear Sir/Madam, Dear Mrs Jones*
> • Order your paragraphs: reason for writing, explaining the situation, what you want to happen
> • Avoid contractions: *I am writing* ... NOT ~~I'm writing~~ ...
> • Use formal expressions: *I contacted* ... NOT ~~I called~~ ...
> • Use passives to avoid being personal: *I was told* ... NOT ~~They told me~~ ...

writing a formal email ■ noun forms of verbs **WRITING** **SKILLS** **9D**

5 Choose the correct options to complete the reply from Suleiman.

To: valerie.lemoir@mailshop.com
Subject: RE: Problems with my order (P389746-D)

¹*Hi Valerie / Dear Ms Lemoir*
I am writing ²*with regard to / about* your email of 29 January.
Firstly, ³*I'm very sorry about / please accept my apologies for* the problems you experienced with our online ordering system, which was ⁴*unacceptable / really bad*. Unfortunately, ⁵*the wrong software was installed / they installed the wrong software* and this has caused some unexpected problems.
Therefore, I ⁶*would be very happy to refund / don't mind refunding* the money, including all delivery costs that ⁷*you were charged / we charged you*. Please ⁸*tell me / advise me of* a suitable date for our delivery team to collect the phone. ⁹*In addition to this / Also*, I would like to offer you a $50-voucher to spend on any product at Phonetastic. I hope this is satisfactory, and we look forward to you shopping with us in future.
¹⁰*Cheers! / With kind regards*,
Suleiman Malik
Customer Services Manager

6 How did Suleiman try to solve the problem? Do you think Valerie will use the company again?

7 A Complete the sentences from Valerie's email with the words in the box. Check your answers in her email.

delivered   delivery   order   ordered

1 I am writing to complain about the problems I have had with my online _____ ..
2 I _____ a red X3 smartphone from your website on …
3 However, the phone was only _____ yesterday – two weeks after I ordered it.
4 Apart from the late _____ , there are …

B How does Valerie repeat her ideas without repeating the exact words?

 Text builder noun forms of verbs

No change: order → order
Noun ends in -ment: argue → argument   **Noun ends in -sion**:   decide → decision
Noun ends in -y: deliver → delivery   **Noun ends in -ation**: inform → information

8 Read the Text builder. Complete the sentences with the noun form of the verbs in brackets.
1 There's a problem with the _____ on this credit card. (pay)
2 We have received your _____ for the job. (apply)
3 In _____ , this is a serious problem. (conclude)
4 I didn't receive an _____ for their mistakes. (apologize)
5 He hasn't given me an _____ yet. (answer)

9 A PREPARE Choose a problem with an online order. Make notes about the details of the problem and what you want the company to do (e.g. contact you/exchange/refund).

missing part   arrived 3 days late   wrong colour   wrong product delivered

B PRACTISE Use the Skill box to write a formal email complaining about the order. Repeat your ideas in different ways using noun and verb forms of words.

C PERSONAL BEST Swap emails with your partner. Tick (✓) three sentences you think are very good. Suggest three ways to improve his/her email.

Personal Best Write the company's reply to your partner's email from exercise 9.

UNIT 10 Sport and fitness

LANGUAGE past perfect ■ sports and competitions

10A Winning is everything

1 ▶10.1 Listen and match the speakers with pictures a–c.

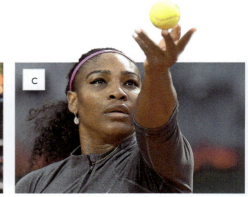

2 ▶10.1 Complete the sentences with the words in the box. Listen again and check.

beat win match race umpire athlete medal trophy score crowd

1 The _____ is almost over. In one minute, Real Madrid will _____ the game and the _____. But wait. What's this? Here come Arsenal. The ball goes to Walcott. He has to _____ a goal, now. He does!
2 Serena Williams to serve. Was that out? She looks at the _____. You can hear the _____ cheering. They're sure Serena is going to _____ her sister, Venus.
3 Here they come, the end of the 100 m _____, and Bolt is going to win the gold _____ again. Yes, he's done it. What an amazing _____!

Go to Vocabulary practice: sports and competitions, page 152

3 Discuss the questions in pairs.

1 Do you prefer to watch or take part in sports?
2 Have you ever won a medal or a trophy?
3 Would you like to be a professional athlete?
4 How have sports changed over the last 100 years?

4 Read the text. What are the names of the athletes in the pictures?

THE TOUGHEST RACE EVER?

There are some difficult events in the Olympic Games, but nothing compares with the 1904 Olympic Marathon. One athlete almost died and the race ended in a public scandal.

The marathon started on an incredibly hot day in St Louis, in the USA, and there were lots of cars and horses on the dusty roads. One athlete, William Garcia, started coughing after he'd breathed in too much dust. It was so bad that he had to give up the race and was taken to hospital. Another runner, Len Tau from South Africa, eventually finished in ninth place, but he was disappointed because some wild dogs had chased him for over a mile in the opposite direction during the race!

Meanwhile, the first athlete to cross the finish line was an American, Fred Lorz. The crowd thought a local athlete had won so they started celebrating, but actually, Lorz had cheated. He'd felt ill during the race and had travelled 11 miles in a car! Fortunately, a spectator had seen Lorz getting out of the car one mile before the finish line and told the referee, so Lorz didn't win the gold medal.

The next runner to finish was another American, Tom Hicks. Hicks hadn't felt well either so his friends had given him a drink of eggs mixed with some chemicals to help him. However, this had made him feel even worse and, in the end, his friends had helped him walk the final part of the race. Even though he hadn't run the whole marathon on his own, the organizers presented Hicks with the gold medal after the hardest marathon of all time.

84

past perfect ■ sports and competitions   LANGUAGE   10A

5 A Read the sentences. Tick (✓) the action that happened first: **a** or **b**?

1 a ☐ William Garcia **started** coughing after   b ☐ he**'d breathed** in too much dust.
2 a ☐ Len Tau **was** disappointed because   b ☐ some wild dogs **had chased** him for over a mile.
3 a ☐ The crowd thought a local athlete **had won**, so   b ☐ they **started** celebrating.
4 a ☐ Even though he **hadn't run** the whole marathon,   b ☐ the organizers **presented** Hicks with the gold medal.

B Look at the verbs in **bold** in exercise 5A and answer the questions. Then read the Grammar box.

1 What tense are the actions that happened first? *past simple / past perfect*
2 What tense are the actions that happened later? *past simple / past perfect*
3 How do we form the past perfect? _____ + _____

Grammar   past perfect

An action that happened before another action in the past:
I **had forgotten** my keys so I couldn't open the door.   I explained to my boss that I **hadn't finished** the report.
Had you **eaten** anything before you went swimming?   When I got to the party, my friend **had gone**.

Go to Grammar practice: past perfect, page 130

6 ▶ 10.6   **Pronunciation:** *'d / hadn't*   Listen to the sentences. How do you say *'d* and *hadn't*? Listen again and repeat.

1 He**'d** breathed in too much dust.   2 He **hadn't** run the whole marathon on his own.

7 A Complete the sentences with the past perfect form of the verbs in brackets.

1 They _____ before the game. (not warm up)   3 She _____ a rugby match before. (not see)
2 I knew they _____! (cheat)   4 We celebrated because he _____ a goal. (score)

B ▶ 10.7   In pairs, say the sentences. Pay attention to the *'d/hadn't* contractions. Listen, check and repeat.

Go to Communication practice: Student A page 164, Student B page 172

8 ▶ 10.8   Complete the text with the correct form of the verbs in brackets. Use the past simple or past perfect. Listen and check.

Who's the twelfth man?

There are eleven players in a football team, but in this team photo of Manchester United there are twelve – so who's the twelfth man? The team [1]_____ (be) very excited after they [2]_____ (travel) to Germany for their Champions League match against Bayern Munich. The players [3]_____ (line up) for a photo when suddenly Karl Power [4]_____ (run) onto the pitch dressed in the Manchester United kit and [5]_____ (stand) next to them. Even though some of the players [6]_____ (notice) Karl, the photographer still [7]_____ (take) the photo. Karl then [8]_____ (go) back to his seat to watch the match. Unfortunately, Manchester United [9]_____ (lose), but Karl was happy because he [10]_____ (meet) his heroes!

9 A In pairs, write as many sentences as you can about the pictures. Use the past simple and past perfect.

He was very disappointed because he'd lost the match.

B Tell the class your most interesting sentence. Who has the most original explanation?

Personal Best   Write about an occasion when you did something that you had never done before.

10 SKILLS READING finding information in a text ■ giving examples

10B Rock 'n' roll on wheels

1 Look at the pictures and the title of the text on page 87. Answer the questions.

1 What are the Paralympic Games?
2 Have you ever seen a wheelchair rugby match?
3 Would you like to take part in a game?
4 What kind of person do you think Laura is?

> **Skill finding information in a text**
>
> **When we want to find information in a longer text, we need to know where to look.**
> - Read the text quickly and understand the general topic of each paragraph.
> - Read the question carefully and underline any key words.
> - Match the question with the paragraph that has the information you need.
> - Read this paragraph in detail to answer the question.

2 Read the Skill box. Then read the text quickly and match paragraphs A–G with topics 1–7.

1 how it feels to play wheelchair rugby _____
2 how to find out more about the sport _____
3 creating interest in disabled sports _____
4 Laura's physical appearance _____
5 media interest in wheelchair rugby _____
6 the origins of the sport _____
7 the rules of wheelchair rugby _____

3 **A** Read the questions. Underline the key words and match them with paragraphs A–G.

	Paragraph	Answer
1 How long does it take Tim to cross the court?	_____	_____
2 Which movie did wheelchair rugby appear in?	_____	_____
3 What other wheelchair sports are there?	_____	_____
4 When was wheelchair rugby invented?	_____	_____
5 What is the official wheelchair rugby organization?	_____	_____
6 Where does Laura have a bandage?	_____	_____
7 How many players are on a wheelchair rugby team?	_____	_____

B Read the paragraphs and answer the questions.

4 Did you know anything about wheelchair rugby before you read the article? Would you like to watch a match?

5 Find the highlighted words in the text.

1 Which words come before nouns?
2 Which words come at the start of a sentence?

> **Text builder giving examples**
>
> **Listing examples:**
> *I'd like to visit countries in south-east Asia, **like** Thailand and Vietnam.*
> *You shouldn't eat unhealthy food, **such as** pizzas or hamburgers.*
>
> **Giving an example phrase:**
> *She's had problems at work. **For example,** she arrived late every day last week.*
>
> **Look!** We can also use **for instance** instead of *for example* with no change in meaning:
> *She's had problems at work. **For instance**, she arrived late every day last week.*

6 Read the Text builder. Complete the sentences with your own ideas. Compare your sentences in pairs.

1 Cheating has become very common in some sports. For example, …
2 My country has produced some famous sportspeople, like …
3 Some sports can be quite dangerous, such as …

7 **A** In pairs, choose an interesting sport. Prepare a short talk about it. Use the ideas in the boxes.

where it is played · the rules · how popular it is · famous players · how it feels to play · media interest

B Tell another pair about your sport. Would you like to try this sport?

86

finding information in a text ■ giving examples READING SKILLS 10B

Sports interview:
Tim White meets wheelchair rugby player, Laura Sabetta

A
The first thing I notice about Laura Sabetta is her arms. They're almost as big as my legs. The next thing I notice is a bandage on her arm. 'I often get injuries because we play to win,' the Argentinian athlete explains, '… it's rugby, after all.'

B
Wheelchair rugby has always been a tough, physical sport. Invented in Canada in 1977, it was first called 'Murderball'. As the sport's popularity grew, the name changed to the more serious 'wheelchair rugby'. It was a new name, but the game was just as violent.

C
People who have never played the sport might think of it as a fun way to spend an afternoon, but it's exhausting. Laura gives me a special wheelchair and I move slowly onto the court. I wear gloves, but it's very hard work pushing the chair using only my arms. Wheelchair rugby is played on a basketball court, which measures 28 x 15 metres, and it takes me over three minutes to cross it. Meanwhile, Laura has already finished warming up.

D
I'm soon happy to join the spectators and watch the match. Wheelchair rugby is a mix of basketball, rugby and ice hockey. Two teams of four players throw and carry a volleyball, trying to score goals. Players score when their wheels cross the line at the end of the court while holding the ball in their hands.

E
Wheelchair rugby's popularity exploded after it featured in the 2005 movie *Murderball*. Many of its players are now big names in Paralympic sports, like the movie's star, Mark Zupan. The sport is now played in more than 25 countries, such as Japan and the USA. So, however you look at it, wheelchair rugby is big news.

F
This places lots of responsibility on the players, as Laura explains. 'There are lots of sports opportunities out there for people who need a wheelchair, such as skiing, tennis and sailing. The important thing is making sure people know about them so they can take part. We also need fans. We want big crowds watching the game. That's why I'm doing this interview!'

G
Getting involved is easy. There's plenty of information online. For example, there's the website of the International Wheelchair Rugby Federation at www.iwrf.com. It's also quite easy to find a match in most large towns if you just want to watch. Many people only watch the sport once every four years at the Paralympic Games, but as Laura tells me, 'For people like me, this isn't a hobby. Since I lost the use of my legs, it's been my life.'

Personal Best Write five more questions about the wheelchair rugby interview.

10 LANGUAGE reported speech ■ parts of the body

10C He said it had changed his life

1 Match the words in the box with the parts of the body.

| chest | knee | shoulder | elbow | neck | wrist |

1 _____   3 _____   5 _____
2 _____   4 _____   6 _____

Go to Vocabulary practice: parts of the body, page 153

2 A Look at the poster. Discuss the questions in pairs.
1 How much exercise do doctors recommend you do each week?
2 Is it possible to get fit doing three minutes of exercise per week?
3 What do you think 'high-intensity training' is?

B ▶ 10.10 Listen to an interview and check your answers.

3 Discuss the questions in pairs.
1 How much exercise do you do per week? What do you do?
2 Do you believe that high-intensity training works? Why/Why not?
3 Would you like to try high-intensity training? Why/Why not?

4 A ▶ 10.10 Complete the sentences about what Carlos and Vicky said. Listen again and check.
1 Carlos said that in HIT you used almost all your _____.
2 Carlos said two years ago he had weighed almost _____ kg.
3 Carlos said he was eating more _____ and _____ now.
4 Carlos said that he had lost _____ kg.
5 Carlos told Vicky that first she would do some gentle cycling to _____.
6 Vicky told Carlos she was going to try _____ seconds of high-intensity cycling.

B Look at the sentences 1–6 again and answer the questions.
1 Which two verbs do we use to report what someone says in the past? _____ _____
2 Which verb do we use when we say who the person is talking to? _____
3 Is it always necessary to use *that* with these verbs? Yes / No

5 A ▶ 10.11 Listen carefully to what Carlos and Vicky said. Write the verbs they used.

1 In HIT, you _____ almost all your muscles.
2 Well, two years ago I _____ almost 100 kg.
3 Oh, and I _____ more fruit and vegetables now.
4 Of course – 75 kg. I _____ 25 kg.
5 OK, so first you _____ some gentle cycling to warm up.
6 Thanks, Carlos. Well, I _____ 20 seconds of high-intensity cycling now.

B Compare the verbs in exercise 5A with the verbs in exercise 4A. How have they changed? Then read the Grammar box.

1 present simple → *past simple*
2 past simple → _____
3 present continuous → _____
4 present perfect → _____
5 will → _____
6 am/are/is going to → _____

88

reported speech ■ parts of the body **LANGUAGE** **10C**

Grammar reported speech

Direct speech:	Reported speech:
'*I **play** tennis.*'	*She said (that) she **played** tennis.*
'*Vicky **tried** HIT.*'	*He said (that) Vicky **had tried** HIT.*
'*It's **raining**.*'	*They said (that) it **was raining**.*
'*She **hasn't arrived** yet.*'	*You said (that) she **hadn't arrived** yet.*
'*I'**ll help** you.*'	*You said (that) you **would help** me.*
'*We'**re going to call** you.*'	*They said (that) they **were going to call** me.*
'*Ravi **can't come** to work.*'	*She said (that) Ravi **couldn't come** to work.*

Look! We use **told** to say who the person talked to: *She **told me** (that) she played tennis.*

Go to Grammar practice: reported speech, page 131

6 ▶ 10.13 Match the sentences in the box with the people. Listen and check.

I go to the gym to meet my friends.   I'll tell my husband because he needs to lose weight.
I can't do HIT at my age!   I've tried it, but I hurt my shoulder.

  Rosa   Kurt   Barry   Jamila

7 ▶ 10.14 **Pronunciation: weak form of *that*** Listen to the sentences. Underline the stressed words. How do we pronounce *that*? Listen again, check and repeat.

1 Carlos said that HIT was very popular.
2 He told me that I should ask some other people what they think.

8 A Complete the sentences using the information from exercise 6.

1 Rosa said that _____.
2 Kurt told Vicky that _____.
3 Barry told her that _____.
4 Jamila said that _____.

B ▶ 10.15 In pairs, practise saying sentences 1–4. Pay attention to the pronunciation of *that*. Listen, check and repeat.

9 In pairs, ask and answer the question *What did ... say?* Use reported speech to answer the questions.

A *What did José say?*   **B** *He said that he ...*

1   I can't go running because I've hurt my ankle.   José
2   Sara   My train is delayed so I'm going to be late.
3   Our teacher is wearing a leather jacket.   Laura
4   David   If you're tired, I'll make you a coffee.

Go to Communication practice: Student A page 164, Student B page 172

10 A In pairs, ask and answer the questions. Make notes of your partner's answers.

1 Have you ever run a long distance?
2 What was the first film you saw at the cinema?
3 What are you going to do this weekend?
4 Can you play any unusual sports?
5 What series are you watching on TV at the moment?
6 What are you doing after the lesson today?

B Work with another student. Report what your first partner said about questions 1–6.

Personal Best Think of a news story or an interview with a sportsperson. Write what the person said.

10 SKILLS SPEAKING making enquiries ■ being helpful

10D Could you tell me …?

1 Discuss the questions in pairs.
1 What are the best ways to keep fit?
2 Have you ever thought about joining a gym?
3 What would be important for you if you joined a gym?
4 Look at the webpage. Would you join this gym? Why/Why not?

2 ▶ 10.16 Watch or listen to the first part of *Learning Curve*. Why does Marc want to join the gym?

3 ▶ 10.16 Watch or listen again and complete the webpage with the correct information.

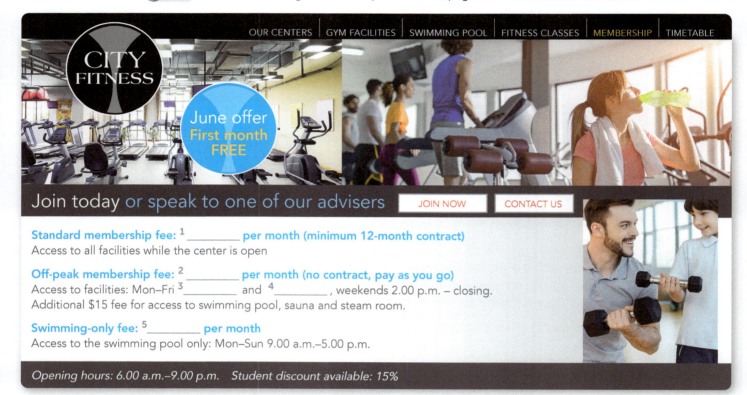

CITY FITNESS

OUR CENTERS | GYM FACILITIES | SWIMMING POOL | FITNESS CLASSES | MEMBERSHIP | TIMETABLE

June offer
First month FREE

Join today or speak to one of our advisers   JOIN NOW   CONTACT US

Standard membership fee: ¹_____ per month (minimum 12-month contract)
Access to all facilities while the center is open

Off-peak membership fee: ²_____ per month (no contract, pay as you go)
Access to facilities: Mon–Fri ³_____ and ⁴_____, weekends 2.00 p.m. – closing.
Additional $15 fee for access to swimming pool, sauna and steam room.

Swimming-only fee: ⁵_____ per month
Access to the swimming pool only: Mon–Sun 9.00 a.m.–5.00 p.m.

Opening hours: 6.00 a.m.–9.00 p.m.   Student discount available: 15%

4 ▶ 10.17 Match the halves to complete Marc's enquiries. Listen and check.

1 Could I speak to someone
2 Could you tell
3 Could you give me some
4 I'd like to ask about
5 Just one more
6 So can I double-check

a the cost, please?
b information about that?
c thing.
d off-peak membership.
e about joining the gym?
f me about the cost?

Conversation builder making enquiries

Starting enquiries politely:
Could I speak to someone about …?
Could you give me some information about …, please?
Excuse me, I was hoping you could help me.

Asking for additional information:
I'd also like to ask about …
I was told … Is that true?
Just one more thing. Do you …?
Can I double-check? Do you …?

5 Read the Conversation builder. Choose three subjects in the boxes. In pairs, make enquiries about City Fitness. Use the information on the webpage to answer.

student discount   opening hours   swimming-only membership
June offer   how to join

making enquiries ■ being helpful   SPEAKING   SKILLS   10D

6 A ▶10.18 Watch or listen to the second part of the show. Does Marc decide to join the gym?

B ▶10.18 Are the sentences true (T) or false (F)? Watch or listen again and check.

1 Marc thought Taylor worked at a different centre. ____
2 Taylor likes this centre because it's small. ____
3 The receptionist told Marc about all the facilities. ____
4 Taylor offers Marc a free training session as a special offer. ____
5 Marc wants to start training slowly. ____

7 ▶10.19 Listen and repeat the receptionist and Taylor's phrases when you hear the beeps. How are they helpful to Marc?

> **Skill** | **being helpful**
>
> There are different ways to be helpful in English, especially with colleagues and customers.
> • Use friendly intonation to show you are happy to help.
> • Make offers and suggestions: *Would you like me to …?   Shall I …?   I'll … if you want.*
> • Check the person is satisfied: *Does that sound OK?   Is there anything else I can help you with?*

8 A Read the Skill box. Are phrases 1–6 answers to questions (A), offers and suggestions (O) or checking the customer is satisfied (C)?

1 The nearest one is on the corner of Sutton Street. ____
2 Do you have any other questions? ____
3 I think it costs about $20 to the city centre. ____
4 I'll just print you a map of the area. ____
5 Would you like me to write that down for you? ____
6 Is there anything else you'd like to know? ____

B ▶10.20 Listen and repeat phrases 1–6. Pay attention to the intonation.

Go to Communication practice: Student A page 164, Student B page 172

9 Discuss the questions in pairs.

1 Have you ever worked with customers or the public? What did you do?
2 What's the most difficult thing about working with customers or the public?
3 Have you ever had a bad experience with customer service? What happened?
4 Can you think of a good experience with customer service? What happened?

10 A PREPARE Choose one of the situations. Use the phrases and your own ideas to prepare questions.

Travel agent
Holidays in the USA
Best city to visit
Cost of flights

Pharmacist
Medicine for the flu
How often to take it
Other advice to feel better

Sports shop assistant
Running shoes
Best type for long distance
Colours and sizes

B PRACTISE In pairs, make enquiries using your questions. Your partner should try to answer your questions and be as helpful as possible.

C PERSONAL BEST Were you a satisfied customer? What could your partner do differently to be more helpful? Choose another situation and make more enquiries.

Personal Best Write down five questions you could ask in a restaurant.

9 and 10 REVIEW and PRACTICE

Grammar

1 Cross (**X**) the sentence which is NOT correct.

1 a I used to have a bike, but then I sold it. ☐
  b I had a bike, but then I sold it. ☐
  c I used to have a bike, but then I used to sell it. ☐

2 a Cervantes wrote Don Quixote. ☐
  b Don Quixote was written by Cervantes. ☐
  c Cervantes was written Don Quixote. ☐

3 a He'd gone home because he'd forgotten his wallet. ☐
  b He went home because he'd forgotten his wallet. ☐
  c He'd forgotten his wallet, so he went home. ☐

4 a Emma said, 'I'll be on time.' ☐
  b Emma told me she would be on time. ☐
  c Emma said me she would be on time. ☐

5 a She didn't used to do much exercise. ☐
  b She didn't do much exercise. ☐
  c She didn't use to do much exercise. ☐

6 a The radio was invented by Marconi. ☐
  b The radio is invented by Marconi. ☐
  c Marconi invented the radio. ☐

7 a He was late because he had missed the bus. ☐
  b He missed the bus, so he was late. ☐
  c He had been late so he had missed the bus. ☐

8 a Pete said he was seeing the film before. ☐
  b Pete said he had seen the film before. ☐
  c Pete said, 'I've seen the film before.' ☐

2 Use the words in brackets to write sentences that mean the same as the first sentence.

1 Someone stole my car last week.
  My car _____ someone last week. (stolen)

2 Neil said, 'I haven't been to Greece.'
  Neil said that _____ to Greece. (been)

3 When I was young I played the piano.
  I _____ the piano. (used)

4 They make Vespas in Italy.
  Vespas _____ in Italy. (are)

5 We ate our soup. Then he brought the drinks.
  When he brought the drinks, we _____ our soup. (had)

6 Kelly said, 'I don't need any help.'
  Kelly _____ any help. (me)

7 I didn't take an umbrella and I got wet.
  I got wet because I _____ an umbrella. (took)

8 I wasn't a very shy child.
  When I was a child, I _____ very shy. (be)

3 Complete the text with the correct form of the verbs in brackets.

HOW NOT TO LOSE YOUR PET

Fumie Takahashi, a 64-year-old woman from Japan, was very happy when the police [1]_____ (tell) her that they [2]_____ (find) her pet parakeet, Piko Chan. But what was amazing was that the bird [3]_____ (tell) the police its own address!

Mrs Takahashi [4]_____ (use / have) another parakeet, but it escaped and flew away. So, when she bought Piko Chan, she taught it to repeat her street name and house number. Last Sunday, Piko Chan escaped, too, when the door to its cage [5]_____ (leave) open. It flew to a nearby hotel and after a few hours, it [6]_____ (take) to the police station by a guest.

The police [7]_____ (say) that the bird [8]_____ (be) silent for two days and they hadn't known what to do with it. Eventually, however, Piko Chan surprised them all when it [9]_____ (tell) them where it [10]_____ (live).

If Piko Chan escapes again, it'll probably be found even more quickly. Its photo has appeared in newspapers all over Tokyo, and Mrs Takahashi recently took the bird to a press conference, where it told journalists its address again.

Vocabulary

1 Put the words in the box in the correct columns.

receipt till ankle crowd knee refund
medal queue referee cheek beat chin

the body	sports	shopping

92

REVIEW and PRACTICE 9 and 10

2 Complete the conversation with the correct words.

Lena These jeans look amazing! Where is the
¹c _hanging_ r_oom_____ ?
Peter Over there, but can you ²a_____ to buy them?
I didn't think you had much money at the moment.
Lena Probably not. I don't ³g_____ p_____
until the end of the month. Can I ⁴b_____
some money from you?
Peter You already ⁵o_____ me 50 euros!
Lena I'll ⁶p_____ b_____ all the money at
the end of the month. I promise.
Peter OK, ⁷t_____ o_____ the jeans. If they
⁸f_____ you, I'll think about it.
Lena Thanks Peter! There's a 70% ⁹d_____ on
them today, they're a real ¹⁰b_____.
Peter OK, Lena.

3 Circle the word that is different. Explain your answer.

1	win	draw	lose	score
2	earn	borrow	lend	pay back
3	bargain	queue	discount	the sales
4	return	exchange	deliver	refund
5	finger	thumb	chest	hand
6	medal	umpire	trophy	race
7	knee	elbow	shoulder	forehead
8	shopping centre	department store	supermarket	changing room

4 Choose the correct word to complete the sentences.

1 I _____ my parents $100.
  a refund **b** owe **c** pay back
2 We _____ them 2–1.
  a won **b** scored **c** beat
3 I'm not buying anything. I'm just _____ .
  a spending **b** getting paid **c** window shopping
4 You can only use your _____ to move the ball.
  a brain **b** heart **c** foot
5 Here's your change and here's your _____ .
  a cash **b** refund **c** receipt
6 There was a _____ of 60,000 at the game today.
  a spectator **b** crowd **c** athlete
7 How much do you _____ in your job?
  a earn **b** be worth **c** borrow
8 You need to _____ before a match.
  a cheat **b** give up **c** warm up
9 Look how long the _____ is!
  a queue **b** till **c** bargain
10 The day after the marathon, my _____ were so tired!
  a back **b** bones **c** muscles
11 When I was younger it was easy to touch my _____ ,
but now I can't.
  a toes **b** fingers **c** thumb

Personal Best

Lesson 9A
Name five things you can do with money.

Lesson 10A
Write a sentence using the past perfect.

Lesson 9A
Write two sentences about your grandparents using *used to*.

Lesson 10A
Name three things you can win.

Lesson 9B
Name five things you usually see in a shopping centre.

Lesson 10B
Write a sentence with *for example*, and another with *such as*.

Lesson 9C
Write a sentence in the present passive, and another in the past passive.

Lesson 10C
Name five parts of the body that we have two of.

Lesson 9D
Name five nouns ending in -*ion*.

Lesson 10D
Give a phrase to start an enquiry, and another to ask for additional information.

Lesson 9D
Write an expression to start a formal email, and another to end it.

Lesson 10D
Give an expression to check someone is satisfied.

93

UNIT 11 At home

LANGUAGE -ing/infinitive verb patterns ■ household objects

11A Dream home

1 Look at the picture. Would you like to live somewhere like this? Why/Why not?

2 Read the text and answer the questions.
1 Where is the house?
2 Who are the people in the picture?
3 Why do they live there?

Living the dream

Have you ever imagined escaping city life and moving to a desert island? Well, meet the family who did just that.

Karyn von Engelbrechten wanted to travel the world after she became tired of her three-hour commute to London, where she worked as an IT manager. She left her job and her home and, with husband Boris and their three children, decided to start a new adventure.

They bought some land on a tiny island in the South Pacific and started to build a house with materials they found on the island. Everything was done by hand. They learned to cut down trees to make floors and doors. Electricity was generated using solar panels and rainwater was collected so the family had water in the bathrooms and kitchen. They even started growing their own fruit and vegetables. Now the family runs their home as a guesthouse for other travellers. If you don't fancy swimming in the beautiful clear ocean, you can sit on the balcony and enjoy watching whales and turtles. The kitchen is basic, but it has most things you'd need, like a fridge-freezer and oven.

There's no air-conditioning, but the bedrooms are cool and comfortable with extra blankets and duvets in the wardrobe for the colder months. From the house, steps go down to your own private beach, or if you're feeling brave, you can explore the island.

It sounds like paradise, but there are some disadvantages. Apart from the fruit and vegetables that Karyn and Boris grow, when they need to buy food the nearest shop is a three-hour boat trip away. The island is also quite near a volcano and they often have earthquakes and tropical storms. And their eldest son, Jack, has gone to school in New Zealand because he missed being with other children his own age.

However, if you're tired of your daily routine, the message is clear – follow your dreams!

3 Which of these things does the house have? *Yes* (✓), *No* (✗) or *Don't know* (?). Read the text again and check.
1 air-conditioning ☐ 3 central heating ☐ 5 freezer ☐ 7 washing machine ☐ 9 oven ☐
2 blankets ☐ 4 dishwasher ☐ 6 wardrobe ☐ 8 duvets ☐ 10 taps ☐

Go to Vocabulary practice: household objects, page 154

4 A Ask and answer the questions in pairs.
1 Do you have a fridge or fridge-freezer at home?
2 How often do you use your washing-machine?
3 How often do you use your iron? Do you like ironing?
4 Do you have a carpet or rugs at home? What colour are they?
5 Do you have a big wardrobe? Is it organized or messy?
6 Do you sleep with a sheet, a blanket or a duvet?
7 Do you have a microwave oven? How often do you use it?
8 Do you use central heating or air-conditioning at home? How often?

B Tell the class some things you found out about your partner.

-*ing*/infinitive verb patterns ■ household objects **LANGUAGE 11A**

5 A Choose the correct form of the verbs to complete the sentences. Check your answers in the text.
1 Have you ever **imagined** *to escape / escaping* city life?
2 Karyn von Engelbrechten **wanted** *to travel / travelling* the world.
3 She **decided** *to start / starting* a new adventure.
4 You can sit on the balcony and **enjoy** *to watch / watching* whales and turtles.

B Answer the questions about the verbs in **bold** in sentences 1–4.
1 Which form of the verb comes after *imagine* and *enjoy*? Infinitive with *to* / *-ing* form
2 Which form of the verb comes after *want* and *decide*? Infinitive with *to* / *-ing* form

6 A Find examples of the verbs in the box in the text. Put them in the correct column.

manage   start   learn   fancy   need   miss

Verbs followed by *-ing*	Verbs followed by the infinitive with *to*

B Which verb can be followed by both the infinitive with *to* and the *-ing* form? _____
Now read the Grammar box.

> **Grammar** *-ing*/infinitive verb patterns
>
> Verbs followed by the *-ing* form: She **enjoys living** in the city.
> Verbs followed by the infinitive with *to*:   I **want to live** in a bigger house.
>
> **Look!** Some verbs can be followed by both the infinitive and *-ing* forms:
> It's started **to rain**. = It's started **raining**.

Go to Grammar practice: *-ing*/infinitive verb patterns, page 132

7 ▶11.4 **Pronunciation:** sentence stress Listen and <u>underline</u> the stressed words in the sentences. How is *to* pronounced? Listen, check and repeat.
1 Karyn wanted to travel the world.
2 She enjoys watching whales and turtles.

8 A Complete the sentences with the correct form of the verbs in brackets.
1 She's planning _____ Science. (study)
2 My doctor suggested _____ less coffee. (drink)
3 I haven't forgotten _____ the customer. (call)
4 Do you fancy _____ tonight? (eat out)
5 We can't afford _____ on holiday. (go)
6 We should spend more time _____ together. (talk)

B ▶11.5 In pairs, practise saying the sentences. Pay attention to the sentence stress. Listen, check and repeat.

Go to Communication practice: page 174

9 A Complete the questions with the correct form of the verbs in brackets.
1 Imagine _____ (design) your dream house. What would you want it _____ (be) like?
2 Do you expect _____ (work) in the same job all your life? Are you planning _____ (change) jobs soon? What do you hope _____ (do) in the future?
3 Do you enjoy _____ (travel)? Have you arranged _____ (go) anywhere soon?
4 Do you like _____ (live) in your house? What would you like _____ (change) about it?
5 Would you like _____ (live) abroad in the future? Where do you fancy _____ (live)?
6 At what age do you think you will stop _____ (work)? What will you spend your time _____ (do) when you retire? Do you think you will miss _____ (work)?

B Ask and answer the questions in pairs.

Personal Best   Write a description of a room in your house including all the things inside it.

95

11 SKILLS LISTENING understanding and interpreting information ■ omission of words ■ housework

11B The truth about housework

1 Look at the picture. Have you ever seen a kitchen like this? If so, where?

2 Complete the man's list of jobs with the words in the box.

do (x3)   clear   take out   load   mop   water

1 _____ the washing up   3 _____ the ironing   5 _____ the table   7 _____ the rubbish
2 _____ the dishwasher   4 _____ the washing   6 _____ the plants   8 _____ the floor

Go to Vocabulary practice: housework, page 155

3 Complete the table about you. In pairs, compare your tables and explain your answers.

Housework I hate doing	Housework I don't mind doing	Housework I enjoy doing

4 A ▶ 11.7   In pairs, decide if the sentences are true (T) or false (F). Watch or listen to the first part of *Learning Curve* and check.

1 It's a fact that everyone hates doing housework.   _____
2 The majority of us usually prefer to do other activities in our free time.   _____
3 Today, robots that can do the housework for us really exist.   _____
4 Robots will never have arms and legs.   _____
5 In Japan, there's a robot which can pick up heavy things.   _____

B ▶ 11.7   Watch or listen again. Write down the key words that Simon or Kate use that helped you check the answers.

Skill   understanding and interpreting information

It's helpful to notice key words and phrases before you listen.
- Look at the questions and underline any key words or phrases.
- Think about other words or phrases that speakers could use to give this information.
- As you listen, pay attention to all the words and phrases you have noticed or thought of.

understanding and interpreting information ■ omission of words ■ housework   LISTENING   SKILLS   11B

5 **A** Look at the underlined key words in questions 1 and 2 and think about what words and phrases Julie might use. Underline the key words in questions 3-6.

B ▶ 11.8 Watch or listen to the second part of the show. Choose the correct options.

1 What does Julie prefer doing at the weekends?
   a She prefers spending time with her children.
   b She prefers going shopping.
   c She prefers doing housework.
2 Why does she want her children to do housework?
   a She has too much work.
   b So they learn to do things on their own.
   c Because it's healthier than videogames.

3 Why did Axel buy a cleaning robot?
   a He wants more time for himself.
   b The salesman offered him a good price.
   c He has injured his back.
4 What does he say about his dishwasher?
   a It's broken.
   b He prefers doing the washing by hand.
   c It works very well.

5 Why does Roberta buy the 'Mop It' robot?
   a It's better at cleaning than she is.
   b Her friend has one.
   c There was a discount.
6 How does housework help her?
   a It's a way to do exercise.
   b It helps her to relax.
   c She saves money.

6 Discuss the questions in pairs.
1 Do you share the housework equally at home?
2 Who does the most housework? Why?
3 Did you do housework when you were a child?
4 Do you think doing housework is good for you?

7 ▶ 11.9 Read and listen to the phrases from the programme. Which words are missing? Why didn't the speakers use them?
1 Just doing a bit of dusting in the studio.
2 Kate, anyone there with an opinion?
3 Makes the floor look good.
4 It does a better job than I can. So exciting!

Listening builder   omission of words

Speakers sometimes don't say all the words in a sentence because they think the meaning is obvious without them, or because they don't want to repeat words or phrases.

Pronouns: *No, (I) don't really like cleaning.*
Articles: *(The) Dishwasher's broken.*
be and auxiliary verbs: *(It's) Time for spring cleaning.*
There is/are: *(Is there) Anyone there with an opinion?*
Avoid repeating words: *It does a better job than I can (do).*
Phrases: *Anyway, (let's go) back to Kate.*

8 **A** ▶ 11.10 Read the Listening builder. Read and listen to the conversation. Which words are missing?

Karim Hi, Maya. ¹_____ You there?
Maya ²_____ In the living room. ³_____ Just clearing the table.
Karim ⁴_____ Coffee's ready. ⁵_____ Want some?
Maya No, thanks. ⁶_____ Already had three ⁷_____ today.

B ▶ 11.11 Listen and check.

9 In pairs, discuss the statement: 'People only notice housework when it isn't done.'

Personal Best Write a short conversation about housework where the speakers omit words.

11 LANGUAGE articles ■ words to describe materials and clothes

11C Technology you can wear

1 Discuss the questions in pairs.
   1 Do you find it difficult to decide what to wear each day?
   2 How often do you buy new clothes?
   3 What are your favourite clothes in your wardrobe?

2 Label the picture with the materials in the box.

   cotton   leather   wood   denim   wool   metal

   Go to Vocabulary practice: words to describe materials and clothes, page 156

3 In pairs, describe the different types of clothes.

   - what you're wearing now
   - what you wear at the weekend
   - what you'd wear at a wedding
   - what you'd wear to a party
   - what you'd wear to a job interview
   - what you'd wear on a first date

4 Look at pictures a–c. What do they show? Read the text and match them with descriptions 1–3.

WEARABLE TECHNOLOGY

Our houses are full of technology, but how much do we have in our wardrobes? You might think you don't have any, but get ready for that to change. Experts predict that the amount of money we spend on wearable technology will reach $74 billion a year by 2025. You're probably already familiar with smart watches and fitness bracelets, but what are some of the other things coming our way?

1 MATERIAL THAT CAN COMMUNICATE

In the USA, Google and Levi's® are developing a new kind of material that is touch-sensitive, like the screen on a smart phone. The material is made by mixing thin metal wires with cotton, denim or silk. Designers can then use this material to create interactive areas on clothes and furniture. Soon people will be able to control machines just by touching their trouser legs!

2 ACCESSORIES THAT CONTROL YOUR TEMPERATURE

Have you ever been in a place where half the people are complaining about the cold, and the other half are too hot? The solution is *Wristify*, a bracelet which can heat or cool your skin at the touch of a button. It's perfect for a trip to the gym, a day at the beach, or for keeping you warm at home, so the bracelet could also save you money on energy bills. The design isn't finished yet, but here's what the final product might look like.

3 CLOTHES THAT CHARGE YOUR PHONE

Pauline van Dongen is an exciting new designer who specializes in wearable technology, and uses both traditional and new materials to create amazing clothes. Her stylish T-shirts and jackets have solar panels, which can charge a mobile phone in just a few hours … when the sun is shining, of course.

5 Discuss the questions in pairs.
   1 Which idea do you think is the most useful? Why?
   2 Would you buy any of these inventions? Why/Why not?
   3 Can you think of other types of wearable technology?

articles ■ words to describe materials and clothes **LANGUAGE** **11C**

6 Complete the sentences with the articles *a*, *an*, *the* or – (no article). Check your answers in the text.

1 The amount of money we spend on wearable technology will reach $74 billion ____ year.
2 People will be able to control ____ machines just by touching their trouser legs!
3 The solution is *Wristify*, ____ bracelet which can heat or cool your skin.
4 Perfect for a trip to ____ gym...
5 ... or for keeping you warm at ____ home.
6 ____ bracelet could also save you money on energy bills.
7 Pauline van Dongen is ____ exciting new designer.
8 ... when ____ sun is shining, of course.

7 Match sentences 1–8 in exercise 6 with rules a–h. Then read the Grammar box.

a We use *a/an* to talk about a person or thing for the first time. ____
b We use *the* when we have already mentioned the person or thing before. ____
c We don't use an article to talk about things in general (plural or uncountable nouns). ____
d We use *a/an* to talk about a person's job. ____
e We use *a/an* in some measurement expressions. ____
f We use *the* if there is only one of the thing. ____
g We use *the* with specific places in a town. ____
h We don't use an article with some places we go to regularly. ____

> 📖 **Grammar** articles
>
> | *a/an* | *the* | No article |
> |---|---|---|
> | I live in **a** tall block of flats. | I live in a modern flat. **The** flat is in ... | They're interested in sports cars. |
> | Eric is **an** architect. | The address is on **the** internet. | I got to work at about 9.00. |
> | We go on holiday twice **a** year. | I'll meet you in **the** park. | |

Personal Best

Go to Grammar practice: articles, page 133

8 A ▶ 11.15 **Pronunciation:** *the* Listen and repeat the phrases. Match the words in **bold** with the sounds /ðə/ and /ðiː/. Why does the pronunciation change?

1 **the** amount of money we spend on technology ____   2 **the** screen on a smartphone ____

B ▶ 11.16 Practise saying the words in pairs. Pay attention to the pronunciation of *the*. Listen, check and repeat.

the solution   the answer   the office   the USA   the internet   the sun   the hour   the gym

Go to Communication practice: Student A page 165, Student B page 173

9 ▶ 11.17 Complete the text with *a*, *an*, *the* or – (no article). Listen and check.

A BRIGHT IDEA

Christina Mercando is ¹____ businesswoman and ²____ inventor. She started ³____ company in ⁴____ USA called Ringly. Her first product is ⁵____ ring that connects to your smartphone. When ⁶____ phone receives ⁷____ text or email, ⁸____ ring lights up. ⁹____ idea came to Christina when she was having ¹⁰____ dinner with friends. She didn't want to miss any important calls on her phone, but she didn't want to put her phone on ¹¹____ dinner table. It's ¹²____ common problem for ¹³____ women who keep ¹⁴____ phones in their handbags or purses, where they may not hear them. ¹⁵____ rings are made in China, and Christina has calls with the factory once ¹⁶____ week. It's ¹⁷____ exciting time for Christina and ¹⁸____ future is definitely bright!

10 In pairs, take turns to talk about these things. Remember to use the correct articles.

types of food and drink you hate

a machine that you couldn't live without

the places you went to yesterday

what you have in your bedroom

some clothes you want to buy but can't afford

how often you charge your mobile phone

Personal Best Think of an idea for another piece of wearable technology. Write about how it could work.

99

11 SKILLS WRITING making writing interesting ■ adjective order

11D House swap

1 Discuss the questions in pairs.
1 Have you ever done a house swap or stayed in someone else's house on holiday?
2 What are the advantages and disadvantages of a house swap?
3 How would you feel about letting strangers stay in your home?

2 Describe the pictures. Which home would you prefer to stay in? Why?

a

b

3 Read the description on a house swap website. Which home from exercise 2 does it describe?

 Homes away from home | Two-bedroom flat in central London, United Kingdom

About our home
Our home is an attractive two-bedroom flat, right in the centre of London. It's a 20-minute walk from the London Eye, where you can see amazing views of the River Thames and the city.

The main bedroom has its own bathroom and a double bed with plain white cotton sheets. Although the second bedroom is slightly smaller, it's bright and has two comfortable single beds. There's a fashionable leather sofa and two large armchairs in the modern living room. The spacious up-to-date kitchen includes everything you'll need, with an electric oven, fridge-freezer, dishwasher and a new Italian coffee machine. Glass doors open from the kitchen onto a gorgeous sunny balcony, where you can have a relaxing breakfast.

The flat is on a peaceful street, but it's just a few minutes away from shops, cafés and some excellent restaurants. The underground station is also close by, so this is an ideal place if you want to explore all of London's attractions.

7 reviews
★★★★

2 bedrooms

Sleeps 4

2 bathrooms

4 A Read the text again. Find words which mean the same as adjectives 1–6.

1 big _____
2 beautiful _____
3 quiet _____
4 very good _____
5 light _____
6 modern _____

B How does the writer make the text interesting? Read the Skill box.

Skill   making writing interesting

We can use different techniques to make our writing more interesting.
- Use a variety of adjectives to describe things: *a **gorgeous**, **sunny** balcony*
- Use synonyms to avoid repeating words: *two **large** armchairs, the **spacious** kitchen*
- Use linkers to give reasons and results (*so, because, that's why*), to contrast information (*but, although, however*) or add information (*and, also, too, as well*).
- When you describe a place, use *where* and an example of what you can do: *a balcony, where you can have a relaxing breakfast*

making writing interesting ■ adjective order **WRITING** **SKILLS** **11D**

5 In pairs, rewrite the sentences to make them more interesting.

1 The house is very pretty. It has a pretty garden.
The house is very pretty and it has a gorgeous garden.

2 The flat is quite small. It's a good place to stay. It's in the centre of the city centre.
_____

3 There's an old living room. It has an old fireplace. You can keep warm in the winter.
_____

4 The building has a quiet roof terrace. You can enjoy nice views of the countryside.
_____

5 If the weather is nice, you can sit in the big garden.
_____

6 Complete the phrases with the adjectives in brackets in the correct order. Check your answers in the text.

1 an _____ _____ flat (two-bedroom, attractive)
2 _____ _____ _____ sheets (cotton, plain, white)
3 a _____ _____ sofa (fashionable, leather)
4 a _____ _____ coffee machine (Italian, new)

Text builder | **adjective order**

When we use more than one adjective to describe a noun, they go in a specific order:
opinion size shape age colour nationality material (noun)
She has long blond hair. NOT ~~She has blond long hair~~.
It's an interesting Chinese painting. NOT ~~It's a Chinese interesting painting~~.

---

7 Read the Text builder. Put the words in the box in the correct columns.

blue Dutch glass green large leather Mexican old
round small square stylish unusual young

opinion	size	shape	age	colour	nationality	material

8 Complete the sentences with the adjectives in brackets in the correct order.

1 We live in a _____ _____ _____ house in the country. (stone, beautiful, old)
2 It's got _____ _____ floors, and is warm and cosy. (wooden, attractive)
3 There's a _____ _____ _____ rug on the floor. (square, wool, large)
4 You can relax on one of our _____ _____ _____ armchairs. (leather, old, comfortable)
5 Outside, there's a _____ _____ garden. (long, beautiful)
6 Near the house, there's a _____ _____ restaurant. (Indian, fantastic)

9 Write descriptions of three items you own, using as many adjectives as possible. Compare with a partner.

I have a beautiful old brown leather armchair.

10 **A** **PREPARE** Plan a description of your home for a house-swap website. Write notes for three paragraphs:

Paragraph 1: the type of home it is and where it is
Paragraph 2: description of the rooms and what is in the rooms
Paragraph 3: description of the local area and what is nearby

B **PRACTISE** Write your description. Remember to make your writing interesting and order adjectives correctly.

C **PERSONAL BEST** Swap your text with a partner. After reading the description, would you like to stay there? How could he/she make the description more interesting?

Personal Best | Write a short description of a place you know well, such as where you work or study, a restaurant or a shop. | 101

UNIT 12 People and relationships

LANGUAGE defining relative clauses ■ relationships

12A Bring your parents to work

1 Match the words in the box with the definitions.

| colleague | neighbour | parents-in-law | boss |
| flatmate | employee | business partner | relative |

1 someone who manages you at work _____
2 your husband's/wife's mother and father _____
3 someone who works for you _____
4 someone in your family _____
5 someone who works with you _____
6 someone who lives near you _____
7 someone who shares a flat with you _____
8 someone who owns a company with you _____

Go to Vocabulary practice: relationships, page 157

2 Choose three of the relationships from exercise 1 and write down the names of people you know. Tell your partner about them.

3 Read the text and answer the questions.

1 Which company introduced the idea of a *Bring Your Parents To Work Day*?
2 How many people in the USA take part in the *Take Your Child To Work Day*?
3 What does the company say the benefits of the day are?
4 How many companies now have a similar day?
5 What does Martin Richards' daughter do at work?

Would you bring your parents to work?

How would you feel about bringing your mum or dad into work with you? Would you be worried about the things that they might say to your boss? Or nervous that they might start showing embarrassing photos of you as a child to the colleague who sits next to you? Well, get ready for *Bring Your Parents To Work Day*, an event which is already becoming popular in some American companies and which could be coming your way soon!

The company where it all started, LinkedIn, realized that there are a lot of parents who don't understand what their children's jobs involve. There is already a national *Take Your Child To Work Day* for workers who want to take their sons and daughters to their places of work, and more than 37 million Americans take part every year. So why not do the same thing for parents? LinkedIn's argument is that employees who are supported by their family are happier and more productive. Now, there are more than 80 companies in 18 countries that organize an annual event for parents to get to know how their kids spend their time at work.

So what do the parents think of it? Martin Richards has just spent a day at the office where his daughter and son-in-law work. 'For me, it was a great opportunity to see how digital marketing works, to meet some of Imogen's co-workers, and – best of all – to spend a day with my eldest daughter!'

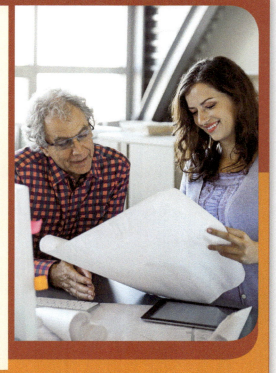

defining relative clauses ■ relationships **LANGUAGE 12A**

4 Discuss the questions in pairs.
  1 As a child, did you ever visit the place where your parents worked? Was it a useful experience?
  2 How would you feel if you brought your parents to your work? Why?
  3 Do you think people's jobs have changed a lot in the last thirty years? If so, how?

5 A Complete the sentences with *who*, *which* and *where*. Check your answers in the text.
  1 Get ready for *Bring Your Parents To Work Day*, an event _____ is already becoming popular in some American companies.
  2 There is already a national *Take Your Child To Work Day* for workers _____ want to take their sons and daughters to their places of work.
  3 Martin Richards has just spent a day at the office _____ his daughter and son-in-law work.

B Look at sentences 1–3 and answer the questions. Then read the Grammar box.
  1 Which word do we use to give information about: people? _____ things? _____ places? _____
  2 In which sentences can we use *that* instead? ____ ____

> **Grammar** defining relative clauses
>
> To give information about people: I'm going to see my cousin **who** lives in Greece.
>   All the employees **that** work in Sales have a meeting.
> To give information about things: The company sells machines **which** are made in Japan.
>   It looks like the shirt **that** my flatmate bought last week.
> To give information about places: That's the restaurant **where** my brother-in-law works.

Go to Grammar practice: defining relative clauses, page 134

6 A ▶12.3 **Pronunciation: sentence stress** Listen to the sentences and underline the stressed words. When do we stress *who*?
  1 Who do you live with?   2 The man who works in the bank.

B ▶12.4 Match the halves to make sentences. Listen, check and repeat. Pay attention to the sentence stress.
  1 A remote control is something which   a young children go.
  2 A flight attendant is someone who   b you use to turn on the TV.
  3 A nursery is a place where   c works on a plane.

7 A Write definitions with *who*, *which* or *where*.
  1 something / use to see small things
  _____
  2 a place / buy newspapers and magazines
  _____
  3 someone / collects the rubbish
  _____
  4 an animal / very slow and lives in trees
  _____
  5 a person / plays an instrument in the street
  _____
  6 a building / horses sleep and eat
  _____

a b c

d e f

B In pairs, match definitions 1–6 with pictures a–f. Do you know the names of these things in English?

Go to Communication practice: Student A page 165, Student B page 173

8 Complete the sentences so that they are true for you. Compare your sentences in pairs.
  1 I like going on holiday to places where …   4 I wouldn't want to live in an area where …
  2 Most of my friends are people who …   5 The worst kind of boss is someone who …
  3 I like TV programmes that …   6 I don't like food which …

  Write about a friend, a relative or a colleague. Use relative clauses to describe him/her.

103

12 SKILLS READING interpreting data ■ expressing approximate quantities

12B In our lifetime

1 In pairs, write down five activities that take up most time in a typical day.
sleeping, working ...

2 Look at Figure 1 on page 105. Answer the questions.
1 What are the top five activities in the pie chart?
2 Are they similar to your list in exercise 1?
3 What information does the pie chart show?
4 Does anything surprise you?

> **Skill   interpreting data**
>
> **Many texts include graphs and charts to show information more clearly.**
> • Read any words on the graphs like the title, the key and the horizontal and vertical axes.
> • Look at the data and think about the information it shows.
> • When you read a paragraph, look at the graph or chart it describes again and see how the words relate to the data.
> • Use information in the text and the graphs and charts to answer the questions.

3 A Read the Skill box. Look at Figures 2 and 3. What do they show?

B Choose the correct options to complete the information about Figures 2 and 3.
1 We spend *more / less* time at work than in the past.
2 Over the last twenty years, there *has / hasn't* been a big change.
3 The total time spent on housework by men and women has *decreased / increased*.
4 Men do *more / less* housework now than in 1965.

4 Read the text and look at Figures 1–3. Tick (✓) the best summary of the text.
1 We have a lot more time to spend with friends and family than in the past. ☐
2 We worked more in the past, but we were happier. ☐
3 We have very busy lives and not much time to do the important things. ☐

5 Read the text and look at Figures 1–3 again. Are the sentences true (T) or false (F)?
1 On average, people live to be 76 years old. ____
2 In 1900, people worked 60 hours a week. ____
3 We spend about a third of our lives sleeping. ____
4 We spend two and a half years in the shower. ____
5 People who work in big cities spend less than a year in their cars. ____
6 We spend a lot of free time using technology. ____

6 Do you think the information is correct for people in your country? Why/Why not? Discuss in pairs.

> **Text builder   expressing approximate quantities**
>
> | | |
> |---|---|
> | Approximately: | In a typical lifetime, we spend **around** 91,000 hours at work. |
> | | People sleep for **about** eight hours a day. |
> | | That means we spend **roughly** three and a half years of our lives studying. |
> | More than: | ... just **over** two years to spend with family and friends. |
> | The same/more: | You can say goodbye to **at least** another year of your life. |
> | Less than: | ... which is **nearly** ten and a half years.   We spend **almost** four years using our phones. |

7 Read the Text builder. Write sentences about how much time you spend doing the activities in the boxes. Use words to express approximate quantities.

sleeping · working · studying · watching TV · going on social media · driving/travelling · talking on the phone · doing exercise · eating and drinking interpreting data ■ expressing approximate quantities   READING   SKILLS   12B

Where does the time go?

Figure 1 How we spend our lives

We have more free time than ever before. In many countries, the average working week is now under 40 hours, far shorter than it was for our parents and grandparents before us. So why do our lives feel so busy, and where does our time go?

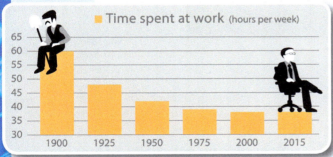

People sleep for about eight hours a day, which means we spend 26 years in our beds over an average lifetime of 78 years. We spend another eleven years watching TV and, depending on where you live, two years of that can be spent just watching the adverts!

In a typical lifetime, we spend around 91,000 hours at work, which is nearly ten and a half years. And do you drive to work? If so, you can say goodbye to at least another year of your life – even more if you work in a big city like Istanbul or Rio de Janeiro and have to sit in traffic jams every day.

In many countries, the law requires young people to stay in education until they're at least 16 years old. Many carry on to further education at university or college. That means we spend on average 31,000 hours – roughly three and a half years of our lives – studying. Two and a half years of our lives are spent in the bathroom – brushing our teeth, using the toilet, having a shower and getting ready to go out. Shopping uses up another two and a half years and we spend at least another four years eating.

The introduction of modern appliances, such as dishwashers, washing machines and microwaves, means that, overall, we spend less time on cooking and cleaning than our parents did. Women still do most of the housework, but men are sharing domestic tasks more than they used to.

In recent years, the big change in how we spend our time is technology. We spend an average of five years online and almost four years using our phones, and those numbers are growing every year. If you add up all that time, it leaves you with just over two years on average to spend with family and friends, to see the world and to achieve your dreams. So, what are you waiting for? The clock is ticking!

Personal Best Make a pie chart and write about how you spend your time at the weekend.

12 LANGUAGE
uses of the *-ing* form and the infinitive with *to* ■ relationship verbs

12C Long-distance love

1 Look at the pictures and the title. Answer the questions in pairs. Then read the text and check.
1 What do you think the text is about?
2 Where do you think the man is?
3 Where do you think the woman is?
4 How do you think they keep in contact?

The ultimate long-distance relationship

Having a long-distance relationship isn't easy. Keeping in touch takes extra effort and not having your partner around when you need support can be difficult. So it's hard to imagine what life is like for Amiko Kauderer, whose boyfriend, Scott Kelly, is often not even on the planet with her. That's because Scott is an astronaut who spends months floating 400 km above The Earth on the International Space Station!

Amiko works at NASA, which is how she got to know Scott. They met a few times, and after talking 'for hours and hours' one evening, Scott finally asked her out. They've now been together for several years. However, Scott's job means he is often away. His first trip to the Space Station lasted six months. After that he lived in space for a whole year to find out what would happen to the human body on a journey to Mars.
On his first trip, it wasn't easy for Amiko to keep in touch. Emailing involved a six-hour delay, but now it's almost instant and it's also possible to videochat once a week. But there are some things that it isn't possible to do. 'One of the things I miss most is holding hands,' says Amiko. 'We can connect on phone calls. I can upload pictures, but you can't upload human touch.'

Other couples might have broken up in such a situation, but not Scott and Amiko. 'We really appreciate a challenge because we know, at the end of it, we can say "Yeah, we did that".'
So whenever you think your love life is difficult, just think of Amiko and Scott!

2 A Match sentences 1–5 with pictures a–e.
1 Amiko **got to know** Scott at a friend's house. ____
2 They **fell in love** at first sight. ____
3 Scott **asked** Amiko **out** on a date. ____
4 **Keeping in touch** now is easier than it was. ____
5 They **broke up**, but **got back together** in the end. ____

B Are the sentences true (T) or false (F)? Check your answers in the text.

Go to Vocabulary practice: relationship verbs, page 157

uses of the *-ing* form and the infinitive with *to* ■ relationship verbs   **LANGUAGE**   **12C**

3 Choose the correct words to complete the sentences. Check your answers in the text.

1 *To have / Having* a long-distance relationship isn't easy.
2 ... after *to talk / talking* 'for hours and hours' one evening, Scott finally asked her cut.
3 He lived in space for a whole year *to find out / finding out* what would happen to the human body.
4 It's also possible *to videochat / videochatting* once a week.

4 Look at sentences 1–4 from exercise 3 again. Complete the rules with the *-ing* form or infinitive with *to*. Then read the Grammar box.

1 We use _____ after an adjective.   3 We use _____ after a preposition.
2 We use _____ as the subject/object of a sentence.   4 We use _____ to say why we did something.

> **Grammar**   **uses of the *-ing* form and the infinitive with *to***
>
> ***-ing* form of the verb:**
> After a preposition: *I'm interested **in learning** languages.*
> Subject/object of a sentence: ***Breaking up** with someone is hard.*   *I hate **breaking up** with someone.*
>
> **Infinitive with *to*:**
> After an adjective: *It's **difficult to meet** new people in this city.   It's **important to keep** in touch.*
> To express a purpose: *I went to Juan's house **to talk** to him.*

Go to Grammar practice: uses of the *-ing* form and the infinitive with *to*, page 135

5 **A** ▶12.7   **Pronunciation:** word stress Listen to the words and <u>underline</u> the stressed syllables. Listen again, check and repeat.

1 distance   2 relationship   3 imagine   4 happen

B ▶12.8   <u>Underline</u> the stressed syllables in the words below. Listen, check and repeat.

important colleagues impossible except technology better afraid probably

6 **A** ▶12.9   Write the infinitive with *to* or the *-ing* form of the verbs in brackets. Listen and check.

1 It's very important _____ with your colleagues at work. (get on)
2 _____ in love at first sight is impossible, except in films. (fall)
3 You can use technology _____ in touch, but meeting face to face is better. (keep)
4 You shouldn't be afraid of _____ someone out. They'll probably say yes! (ask)

B In pairs, practise saying sentences 1–4. Say if you agree or disagree with the sentences.

Go to Communication practice: Student A page 165, Student B page 173

7 Complete the text with the infinitive with *to* or the *-ing* form of the verbs in the box

arrive choose say make show

HOW TO SUCCEED ON A FIRST DATE

1 _____ a nice place to meet is the first thing you need to think about.
2 You should wear nice clothes _____ a good impression.
3 It's important _____ on time.
4 Don't be afraid of _____ the real you.
5 Before _____ goodnight, tell him/her that you enjoyed the date.

8 In pairs, think of more advice for how to succeed on a first date. Use the ideas in the boxes.

be polite   don't talk too much   ask questions   keep eye contact   laugh   listen   smile   tell a joke   relax

A *I think it's important to be polite.*   **B** *Yes, but being polite isn't the most important thing ...*

Personal Best   Write a paragraph about a couple you know. Explain how they met and their relationship.

12 SKILLS SPEAKING giving thanks ■ responding modestly

12D Thanks a million!

1 A Look at the pictures. How are the people celebrating their birthdays?

B Answer the questions.
1 How important are birthdays to you? Why?
2 How did you celebrate your last birthday?
3 What's the best birthday present you've ever received? Why?
4 Have you ever had a surprise birthday party? Did you enjoy it?

2 ▶ 12.10 Watch or listen to the first part of *Learning Curve*. Are the sentences true (T) or false (F)?
1 Today is Simon's birthday. ____
2 Everyone has forgotten about his birthday. ____
3 Simon has a tennis match today. ____
4 Kate gives Simon a present. ____
5 Simon will pay to post the parcel. ____
6 Simon's parents always call him in the morning. ____

3 A ▶ 12.10 Watch or listen again. Match the phrases 1–5 with the reasons a–e.
1 That's very kind of you.   a Kate gives Simon a cup of tea.
2 Thanks a lot.   b Kate offers to make Simon a tea.
3 Thanks so much!   c Simon says he'll pay at the post office.
4 Thanks a million!   d Simon agrees to post a parcel.
5 I will, thanks.   e Kate wants Simon to say hello to his parents for her.

B Look at phrases 1–5 again. Answer the questions.
1 Which phrases are polite responses to something small? ____ ____
2 Which phrases are to say thanks for something special or a big effort? ____ ____ ____
3 Can you think of any other ways to thank someone?

Conversation builder   giving thanks

To be polite:	For a special favour:	To be more formal:
Thanks a lot.	That's very kind of you.	I can't thank you enough.
Thanks very much.	Thanks a million.	I'm so grateful to you.
Thanks.	Thank you so much.	We really appreciate it.

4 ▶ 12.11 Read the Conversation builder. In pairs, read out the sentences and thank your partner in a suitable way. Listen and compare your answers.

1 Here's your T-shirt and $1 change.
2 We've decided to give you a 30% pay rise.
3 Here are some flowers. I know you've been ill.
4 The bus station? It's just across the road.
5 I've done all the shopping for you.
6 I cooked lamb curry. It's your favourite.

108

giving thanks ■ responding modestly **SPEAKING** SKILLS **12D**

5 ▶ 12.12 Watch or listen to the second part of the show. What other ways of thanking people do you hear?

6 ▶ 12.12 Answer the questions. Watch or listen again and check.
1 Who cooked the food for the party? _____
2 Who sent flowers, chocolate and biscuits? _____
3 Did Kate organize the party on her own? _____
4 Whose parents arrive at the party? _____

7 ▶ 12.13 Complete the sentences with the phrases in the box. Listen, check and repeat after the beeps.

it was easy   Glad you noticed   You're welcome   I had help   it isn't a problem

1 **Kate**   Oh, and thanks again for taking this parcel.
  Simon Right. Really, _____ .
2 **Simon** And you look great, Pen. Is that a new dress?
  Penny Thanks. _____ !
3 **Kate**   Jack, you really made a fantastic meal!
  Jack   Oh, come on, _____ . I make this all the time.
4 **Simon** Lovely. I'm so grateful to you both!
  Penny It was nothing. _____ .
5 **Simon** That was a fantastic surprise. Kate, did you do all this by yourself?
  Kate   No, _____ !

🔧 **Skill**   responding modestly

We often respond to congratulations, thanks and compliments in a modest way.
• For congratulations, you can say it wasn't important or hard work, e.g. *It was nothing. I was just lucky.*
• For thanks, you can say it was something small or you enjoyed doing it, e.g. *No problem. It was a pleasure. You're welcome.*
• For a compliment, you can thank the person and say you are pleased, e.g. *Thanks. I'm glad you like it.* You can also say it isn't as good as the person thinks, e.g. *This old thing? I've had it for years.*

8 ▶ 12.14 Read the Skill box. Match phrases 1–6 with responses a–f. Listen and check.
1 I can't thank you enough.
2 I love your new hairstyle.
3 This chicken is delicious.
4 You passed! Congratulations.
5 Thanks for looking after my children.
6 Well done on your promotion.

a Really? I thought it was a bit too spicy.
b Oh, it's just an internal one.
c Thanks. I'm glad you noticed.
d It was a pleasure. They're lots of fun!
e Thanks. The exam wasn't that difficult.
f It's no problem at all.

Go to Communication practice: Student A page 165, Student B, page 173

9 A PREPARE In pairs, look at the pictures and choose a situation. Prepare a short conversation between the people.

 a   b   c   d

B PRACTISE Act out your conversation to another pair.

C PERSONAL BEST What was good about the other pair's conversation? What could they do better? Swap partners and prepare a conversation for another situation.

Personal Best Write a list of people you have thanked this week and explain why you thanked them.

11 and 12 REVIEW and PRACTICE

Grammar

1 Choose the correct options to complete the sentences.

1 Keven has decided _____ his job.
  a leave
  b to leave
  c leaving

2 I normally go to _____ bed at 11.00 p.m.
  a a
  b the
  c – (no article)

3 Do you want _____ out tonight?
  a go
  b to go
  c going

4 My sister is _____ lawyer.
  a a
  b the
  c – (no article)

5 I'm meeting a colleague _____ has just left the company.
  a where
  b which
  c who

6 I phoned him _____ a meeting.
  a arrange
  b to arrange
  c arranging

7 This is the café _____ we said we would meet.
  a where
  b which
  c that

8 I'm keen on _____ to other countries.
  a travel
  b to travel
  c travelling

2 Complete the sentences with the correct form of the verbs in the box.

| remember take buy find |
| go work meet write |

1 I went to the library _____ a book about pets.
2 I'm not happy about _____ late this week.
3 He forgot _____ his girlfriend a birthday present.
4 I've finally finished _____ my essay.
5 I can't stand _____ trains. They're so crowded.
6 She's suggested _____ to the cinema tonight.
7 It's important _____ to turn off this machine when you leave.
8 _____ you is the best thing that has happened to me!

3 Choose the correct options to complete the text.

Stephanie is ¹a / - / the wedding planner and she is ²an / - / the owner of *Blissful Days*, ³a / - / the company based in Sydney, Australia.

How did you become a wedding planner?

I've always loved ⁴go / to go / going to weddings. It's so exciting ⁵see / to see / seeing everyone dressed up and enjoying such a wonderful day. But I noticed that some people couldn't enjoy it because they were worried about ⁶organize / to organize / organizing everything. That's when I realized that I could start a company ⁷which / who / where helps people to plan their weddings.

What advice can you give to couples planning a wedding?

First of all, you should agree on the guests ⁸which / who / where you're going to invite. Once you know how many people will be there, you can find a place ⁹who / which / where everyone will be comfortable. Send out invitations at least six months before the wedding, but expect about 20% of people not to be able to come. This can be more if the date of your wedding is on or near ¹⁰a / - / the public holiday – so always check your dates carefully.

Vocabulary

1 Match the words in the box with the definitions.

| oven get back together plain do the washing |
| hang out the clothes groom stylish iron |
| go out together flatmate |

1 a machine you use to make clothes flat _____
2 a man who is going to get married _____
3 to start a relationship with someone _____
4 simple, with no pattern or design _____
5 someone who you live with _____
6 a machine which you use to cook food _____
7 to dry clothes after you wash them _____
8 to wash your clothes _____
9 fashionable and elegant _____
10 to return to a relationship with someone _____

REVIEW and PRACTICE — 11 and 12

2 Circle the words that are different. Explain your answers.
1 employer   classmate   colleague   business partner
2 break up   fall in love go on a date   go out together
3 oven   dishwasher   wash basin   washing machine
4 mop   sweep   iron   vacuum
5 loose   wool   tight   casual
6 bride   girlfriend   stepsister   father-in-law
7 smart   cotton   denim   silk
8 sheets   pillow   duvet   iron
9 on well   married   in love   back together
10 wash up   lay the table make the bed load the dishwasher

3 Choose the correct word to complete the sentences.
1 My uncle's daughter is my _____ .
   a niece   b cousin   c stepsister
2 I am _____ . I don't have any brothers or sisters.
   a an only child   b a single parent   c a relative
3 I left my job because I _____ badly with my boss.
   a got back   b got on   c went on
4 He _____ on a date!
   a introduced   b asked me out   c kept in touch
5 The _____ is broken. Can you call a plumber?
   a oven   b tap   c fridge-freezer
6 We need new _____ for the bed.
   a rugs   b carpets   c sheets
7 I don't know him. He's a complete _____ .
   a twin   b enemy   c stranger
8 It's really hot today. Can you _____ the plants?
   a sweep   b dust   c water

4 Complete the conversation with the words in the box.

   get to know   break up   vacuum
   introduce   stylish   do   silk   mop

Sue When did you ¹_____ with Harry?
Jo   Two months ago.
Sue Let me ²_____ you to Lee. I'm meeting him tonight.
Jo   I can't. I've got to ³_____ the carpets and ⁴_____ the floor.
Sue You can do that any time!
Jo   But I haven't got anything to wear. I need to ⁵_____ the washing!
Sue Is your ⁶_____ dress clean?
Jo   Yes, it is.
Sue Well, that's really ⁷_____ . Wear that! Come on, you should ⁸_____ him. He's lovely!
Jo   OK, I'll come with you.

Personal Best

Lesson 11A Name five objects you find in a kitchen.

Lesson 12A Write down five people and say how you are related to each of them.

Lesson 11A Name five verbs which are followed by the -ing form.

Lesson 12A Write three sentences with relative clauses and who, which and where.

Lesson 11B Name five housework tasks you do at home.

Lesson 12B Write three sentences using roughly, at least and almost.

Lesson 11C Write a sentence with a/an, and another with the.

Lesson 12C Write a sentence with the infinitive with to.

Lesson 11C Use adjectives to describe two things you are wearing now.

Lesson 12D Give three expressions to thank someone.

Lesson 11D Describe a noun using three adjectives in the correct order.

Lesson 12D Give an expression for responding modestly when someone thanks you.

GRAMMAR PRACTICE

7A Present perfect with *just, yet* and *already*

We often use the present perfect with *just, yet* and *already*.

Have you been to the new café yet?
Yes, I've just/already been there.
No, I haven't been there yet.

We use *just* to talk about something that happened very recently. *Just* comes before the main verb.

Is Andrea at home?
She's just gone to the shops, I'm afraid.

We use *yet* in negative sentences and questions to talk about something that we expected to happen before now. *Yet* comes at the end of the sentence or question.

Have you written the report yet?
I haven't finished it yet.

We use *already* to talk about something that happened before now or earlier than we expected. *Already* comes before the main verb.

Do you want to go out for lunch?
No, thanks. I've already eaten.

We form the present perfect with the verb *have* and the past participle of the main verb. For a full list of irregular verbs, see page 175.

▶ 7.2	I / you / we / they	he / she / it
+	I**'ve just seen** Claudia in the post office. We**'ve already heard** the news.	Kismet **has just bought** a new handbag. The train **has already left** the station.
-	They **haven't found** the keys **yet**.	He **hasn't paid** the bill **yet**.
?	**Have** you **been** to the shops **yet**?	**Has** she **spoken** to the police **yet**?
Y/N	Yes, I **have**. / No, I **haven't**. / **Not yet**.	Yes, she **has**. / No, she **hasn't**. / **Not yet**.

> **Look!** In American English, we often use *just, yet* and *already* with the past simple.
> *I just finished my lunch.*
> *Did Helena call you yet?*
> *The supermarket didn't open yet.*
> *We already gave him the papers.*

1 Complete the conversation with the words in the box.

> just   already   yet (x2)

A Watching TV again? What about your homework?
B I've ¹_____ done it.
A When did you do it?
B On the bus from school ... so now I'm watching the match.
A The match? Has it started ²_____?
B Yes! It's ³_____ started, so you haven't missed anything ⁴_____.
A Great! Let me sit down. I want to watch this, too!

2 Choose the correct words to complete the sentences.

1 Shall we eat out tonight? They've *just / yet / already* opened a new restaurant near us.
2 **A** I have to clean the kitchen tonight.
  B Don't worry. I've *just / yet / already* cleaned it this week.
3 **A** Has Flora passed her driving test *just / yet / already*?
  B Yes, and she only had five lessons!
4 **A** Can I speak to Julia, please?
  B She was here a moment ago, but I think she's *just / yet / already* left the office.
5 Teresa hasn't booked her flight *just / yet / already*. It will be very expensive!
6 **A** Shall we watch *Titanic* tonight?
  B Do we have to? I've *just / yet / already* seen it about twenty times!
7 **A** Excuse me, where's the city centre?
  B Follow the new signposts. They've *just / yet / already* been put up to help tourists.
8 Have you used the new bike lane *just / yet / already*? It's much safer.
9 **A** I think we need to fill up the car with petrol.
  B It's OK. I've *just / yet / already* been to the petrol station today.
10 He only joined the company a year ago and they've *just / yet / already* promoted him twice!

3 Make sentences using *just, yet* or *already*.

1 she / not pack / her suitcase (yet)
_____

2 the neighbours / send us / a party invitation (just)
_____

3 the game / start (already)
_____

4 you / speak / to Charles? (yet)
_____

5 I / buy / a new flat (just)
_____

6 I / have / three cups of coffee today (already)
_____

124

◀ Go back to page 59

GRAMMAR PRACTICE

7C Present perfect with *for* and *since*

We use the present perfect with *for* and *since* to talk about a situation that started in the past and is still true now.

How long have you lived in Brazil? NOT *How long are you living in Brazil?*
I've lived here all my life. NOT *I'm living here all my life.*

We use *since* to refer to a fixed point in time in the past when the situation started.

I've worked for this company since 2010.
I haven't spoken to Farah since last summer.
Have you known Mark since you were a child?

We use *for* to refer to the period of time the situation has been true.

Youssef has been a teacher for two months.
This computer hasn't worked for years!
Has the building been here for a long time?

We use *How long ...?* to ask about the length of time a situation has been true.

How long have you known your boyfriend?
We've known each other since last March.
How long has he been a doctor?
He's been a doctor for about two years.

We form the present perfect with the verb *have* and the past participle of the main verb. For a full list of irregular verbs, see page 175.

▶ 7.12	I / you / we / they	he / she / it
+	I**'ve lived** in this part of the city **for** two years. They**'ve worked** together **since** 1990.	Sam**'s had** this car **for** over 20 years. It**'s been** much hotter **since** last weekend.
−	We **haven't spoken** to each other **for** a year. I **haven't swum** in the sea **since** I was a child.	Isabella **hasn't worn** her glasses **for** ages. He **hasn't driven** a car **since** he had the accident.
?	**How long have** you **known** her?	**How long has** he **been** a teacher?

Present perfect or past simple

We use the past simple to talk about completed actions in the past. We can often give the same information in two different ways.

a period of time / an unfinished action	a point in the past / a completed action
I've lived in Turkey for ten years.	I moved to Turkey ten years ago.
Jo has known me since I was 16 years old.	Jo met me when I was 16 years old.
How long have you worked here?	When did you start working here?
I haven't eaten meat since 2010.	I gave up meat in 2010.

We use the past simple to talk about a time period that started and finished in the past.

How long did you live in Egypt?
I lived there for ten years.
I lived there from 1980 to 1990.
= I don't live there now.

How long have you lived in Mexico?
I've lived here for almost ten years.
I've lived here since 2010.
= I live here now.

---

1 Put the times in the box in the correct column: *for* or *since*.

> 1997   9.30 a.m.   a couple of hours   a few seconds
> a fortnight   a long time   ages   April   five months
> he was a child   I left university   last night
> most of my life   my accident   seventeen years
> several weeks   the middle of June   the weekend
> three centuries   Thursday

for	since

2 Write sentences using the present perfect form of the verbs in brackets. Write one sentence with *for* and one with *since*.

1 I moved to Istanbul in the middle of July. It's the middle of December now. (live)
  I've lived in Istanbul for five months.
  I've lived in Istanbul since the middle of July.

2 I bought my own car when I was 19. I'm 23 now. (have)
  _____
  _____

3 The last time I was on an aeroplane was in August. That was six months ago. (not be)
  _____
  _____

4 I met my best friend when I was five. I'm 22 now. (know)
  _____
  _____

5 I gave up English in 2005. That was ages ago. (not study)
  _____
  _____

3 Choose the correct form of the verbs to complete the sentences.

1 He *didn't speak* / *hasn't spoken* to his mum since he *got back* / *'s got* back from his holiday.
2 I *bought* / *'ve bought* this car in 2007, so I *'m having* / *'ve had* it for more than ten years now.
3 I'm a sales manager and I *worked* / *'ve worked* in this department for two years. Before that, I *worked* / *'ve worked* in marketing from 2012 to 2015.
4 We *knew* / *'ve known* each other for about ten years, in fact since we *met* / *'ve met* at university.
5 I *was* / *'ve been* worried about Frank since he *lost* / *'s lost* his job.
6 He *lost* / *'s lost* his phone this morning so I *'m not speaking* / *haven't spoken* to him for a few hours now.
7 I *lived* / *'ve lived* in Chicago for two years, but then I *moved* / *'ve moved* to Washington DC and I *lived* / *'ve lived* here since then.
8 Their wedding *was* / *has been* in May, so they *are* / *'ve been* married for nearly six months now.

◀ Go back to page 62

125

GRAMMAR PRACTICE

8A *too, too many, too much* and *(not) enough*

We use *too, too many* and *too much* to mean 'more than necessary' or 'more than is good'.

This exam is too difficult. There are too many questions!

We use *too* before adjectives and adverbs.

That restaurant is too expensive.
She works too hard.

We use *too many* before countable nouns.

I drink too many cups of coffee.

We use *too much* before uncountable nouns.

I eat too much chocolate.

We can also use *too much* after a verb without an object.

He worries too much.

We use *enough* to mean 'the right amount' or 'sufficient'. We can also use *not enough* to mean 'less than necessary' or 'less than is good'.

Is your coffee sweet enough? I didn't have enough sugar for everyone.

Enough comes before countable and uncountable nouns.

He doesn't eat enough vegetables.
Have we got enough time?

Enough comes after an adjective or adverb.

The information isn't clear enough.
He didn't sing well enough to win the competition.

We can also use *enough* after a verb without an object.

I didn't sleep enough last night.

▶ 8.2	too / too many / too much	(not) enough
Countable nouns	You shouldn't watch **too many films**.	We have **enough eggs** to make two cakes.
Uncountable nouns	Jen drinks **too much coffee** in the morning.	Do you have **enough money** to buy those shoes?
Adjectives	The train is **too crowded** at rush hour.	The soup is**n't hot enough**.

1 Choose the correct words to complete the sentences.

1 She eats *too much / too many* sweets.
2 They don't eat *enough vegetables / vegetables enough*.
3 Our flat is *too much / too* small for a party.
4 He has *too much / too many* sugar in his coffee.
5 Are you sure you're *fit enough / enough fit* to run a marathon?
6 You eat *too much / too many* junk food.
7 I don't have *enough money / money enough* to buy a new car.
8 These jeans are *too much / too* big for me now that I've lost weight.

2 Complete the sentences using *too, too many, too much* and *enough*.

1 You eat _____ takeaway meals. Don't you ever cook?
2 Don't cook the broccoli for _____ long.
3 My English isn't good _____ to have a conversation.
4 You drink _____ coffee. It isn't good for you.
5 I don't earn _____ money to buy a house.
6 I'm _____ tired to go out tonight.
7 My son spends _____ time playing computer games.
8 I have a stomach ache. I ate _____ cakes.

3 Rewrite the sentences using the words in brackets.

1 You should do more exercise. (enough)
   You don't do enough exercise.
2 You eat more sugar than you should. (much)
   _____
3 She's too young to drive. (old)
   _____
4 It isn't quiet enough to work. (noisy)
   _____
5 We need more petrol. (enough)
   _____
6 There are more cars on the road than there should be. (too)
   _____

◀ Go back to page 67

8C must(n't) and (not) have to

We use *must* and *have to* to talk about obligations and rules.

You must always lock the door when you leave.
Amy has to wear smart clothes at work.

When we ask questions about obligations and rules, we usually use *have to*.

Do you have to start work early?
Why do we have to park the car here?

We use *mustn't* to talk about things that are not allowed. We call this prohibition.

I mustn't eat any chips. I'm on a diet.
You mustn't start the exam until I say.

We use *don't have to* to say that something isn't necessary.

You don't have to speak English for this job, but it's useful.
Kasim doesn't have to work today. It's a holiday.

▶ 8.9

	I / you / we / they	he / she / it
have to	**I have to work** late tonight again, unfortunately. Do you **have to take** the train today? Yes, I **do**. / No, I **don't**.	Jackie **has to study** Maths at school. Does he **have to wait** for a long time? Yes, he **does**. / No, he **doesn't**.
must	We **must** all **eat** healthier food.	Karima **must do** her exams again.
not have to	You **don't have to pay** – it's free!	He **doesn't have to wear** a uniform at school.
mustn't	I **mustn't be** late for the meeting.	Luke **mustn't eat** too much salt.

Look! *Must* and *have to* often have a similar meaning.
I must go to the doctor.
I have to go to the doctor.

However, *mustn't* and *don't have to* have different meanings.
You mustn't walk on the grass. = it's not allowed.
You don't have to walk on the grass – you can walk on the path. = it's not necessary. You can choose.

1 Make sentences using the positive (+), negative (–) or question form (?) of *have to*.

1 What time / you / arrive / at the station (?)
   _____
2 My sister / study / English / at school (+)
   _____
3 You / show / your passport / to enter the country (–)
   _____
4 Lenny / cook / dinner / tonight (?)
   _____
5 We / finish / the project / until next week (–)
   _____
6 You / drive / on the left / in the UK (+)
   _____

2 Choose the correct words to complete the conversation.

A What's wrong, Urs?
B My brother ¹*mustn't / has to* go to the hospital tomorrow.
A Oh no! Why does he ²*must / have to* go?
B It's nothing serious. He ³*has to / mustn't* have a blood test.
A Does he ⁴*have to / has to* spend the night there?
B No, he ⁵*hasn't / doesn't*. The worst thing is he ⁶*doesn't have to / mustn't* eat anything for 24 hours.
A I ⁷*don't have to / mustn't* work tomorrow. I can give him a lift to the hospital, if you want.
B Thanks, Ada. That's great. He ⁸*mustn't / must* be there at 10.00 a.m.
A That's fine.
B Great, he'll be happy he ⁹*mustn't / doesn't have to* take the bus ... especially without any breakfast!

3 Look at the poster. Complete the rules for the swimming pool with the verbs in brackets.

1 Adults _____ (pay) to use the pool.
2 Children _____ (pay) to go swimming.
3 You _____ (eat) by the pool.
4 You _____ (have) a shower before you swim.
5 You _____ (run) near the pool.

◀ Go back to page 71

GRAMMAR PRACTICE

9A *used to*

We use *used to* + infinitive to talk about habits or situations that were true in the past, but aren't true now.

I used to cycle to school every day. = I don't cycle to school now.
I used to live in a small town. = I don't live there now.

We form the negative with *didn't* + *use to* + infinitive.

I didn't use to drink so much coffee. (=I drink a lot now).
She didn't use to like spicy food. (=She likes it a lot now).

We form questions with *did* + *use to* + infinitive.

Did you use to play in the school football team?
Why did you use to have two cars?

We can use the past simple instead of *used to*. The meaning is the same.

I used to have English classes at school = I had English classes at school.
She used to be shy when she was younger = She was shy when she was younger.

We don't use *used to* to talk about actions that only happened once.

I bought this shirt last year. NOT ~~I used to buy this shirt last year.~~
They started work at 9.00 this morning. NOT ~~They used to start work at 9.00 this morning.~~

▶ 9.1	I / you / he / she / it / we / they
+	I **used to like** reggae music when I was a teenager.
−	He **didn't use to be** as rich as he is now.
?	**Did** you **use to go** to the beach every day when you lived in Greece?
Y/N	Yes, I **did**. / No, I **didn't**.

Look! *Used to* only refers to the past. We use *usually* + present simple to talk about habits and situations which are true now.
Hande usually gets the bus to work.
He's not usually late for class.
How do you usually contact your family?

---

1 Read the text. Write sentences with *used to* or *didn't use to* and the verbs in brackets.

He used to be rich!

George Kaltsidis lives in a small house in the north of England. He drives an old Ford Fiesta and wears a second-hand watch. However, believe it or not, George used to be a millionaire and lived a life of luxury. He wasn't happy and last year he gave all his money away to charity. He's much happier now, he says. But what did his life use to be like?

1 He (live) in a small house. He (live) in an expensive apartment.
He didn't use to live in a small house. He used to live in an expensive apartment.

2 He (drive) an old car. He (have) a new BMW.
_____

3 He (be) quite lonely because he (see) his family or friends very much.
_____

4 He (wear) expensive clothes and he never (buy) second-hand things.
_____

5 He (go) on luxury holidays, but he (enjoy) himself.
_____

2 Complete the sentences with the positive, negative or question form of *used to* and the verbs in the box.

have (x2)   do   work   argue   go   like   be

1 They _____ a house in Spain, but they sold it last year.
2 _____ you _____ a lot of sport when you were younger?
3 I _____ to the gym, but now I usually go three times a week.
4 _____ you _____ a lot with your parents?
5 Where _____ you _____ before you got this job?
6 She _____ long hair, but now she prefers it short.
7 I _____ fish, but I love it now.
8 There _____ a park here before they built those houses.

3 Complete the sentences with *used to* or the past simple form of the verbs in brackets if *used to* is not possible.

1 Did you _____ a school uniform? (wear)
2 I _____ my arm when I was eight. I was ten. (not break)
3 I _____ quite naughty at school. (be)
4 My parents _____ a lot of money. (not earn)
5 I _____ a £50 note in the street one day. (find)
6 My grandma _____ listening to the radio. (love)
7 I _____ a lot of computer games when I was a teenager. (play)
8 The first film I _____ at the cinema was *Titanic*. (see)

◀ Go back to page 77

GRAMMAR PRACTICE

9C The passive

Sentences can be either active or passive.

Active: *My brother wrote this book.*
Passive: *This book was written by my brother.*

We use the active sentence to focus on the person who does the action.

My brother wrote this book.

We use the passive sentence to focus on the action itself or on the thing the action affects.

This book was written by my brother.

We also use the passive when we don't know who does/did the action or it isn't important.

These coffee machines are made in Italy.
My wallet was stolen yesterday.

We form the present simple passive with *am/is/are* + past participle of the main verb.
We form the past simple passive with *was/were* + past participle of the main verb.

Present passive: *Toyota cars are built in Japan.*
Past passive: *The buildings were destroyed five years ago.*

To say who does/did the action, we use *by*.

Lots of hotel towels are taken by tourists as souvenirs.
This building was designed in 1985 by a Chinese architect.

To form questions, we put the verb *be* before the subject.

Is your watch made of gold?
When was the book written?
Who was the music sung by?

▶ 9.12	Present passive	Past passive
+	The football matches **are played** in the evening.	The film **was directed** by Steven Spielberg.
−	The painting **isn't signed** by the artist.	Chess **wasn't invented** in Europe.
?	**Are** these biscuits **made** with butter?	**Were** the workers **paid** last month?
Y/N	**Yes**, they **are**. / **No**, they **aren't**.	**Yes**, they **were**. / **No**, they **weren't**.

1 Write sentences in the present or past simple passive.
  1 English / speak / here (present)
    English is spoken here.
  2 This guitar / play / by Jimi Hendrix (past)
    _____
  3 The soup / make / with fresh vegetables (present)
    _____
  4 When / the photos / take? (past)
    _____
  5 Who / the film / direct / by? (past)
    _____
  6 credit cards / not accept / here (present)
    _____

2 Rewrite the sentences in the passive.
  1 More than 162 million people use eBay.
    eBay _____ .
  2 The Channel Tunnel connects Britain and France.
    Britain and France _____ .
  3 Facebook bought WhatsApp for $22 billion.
    WhatsApp _____ .
  4 Steven Spielberg didn't direct *Jurassic World*.
    Jurassic World _____ .
  5 They make sushi with rice and raw fish.
    Sushi _____ .
  6 Did Tolstoy write *War and Peace*?
    Was _____ .

3 Complete the text with the active or passive form of the verbs in brackets.

HIDDEN TREASURE

Treasure Detectives is a British TV show and it ¹____ (watch) by more than 300,000 viewers. Each week, two different objects ²____ (examine) very carefully by experts to find out if they are valuable treasures or copies of original works.

Robert Darvell ³____ (contact) the programme and ⁴____ (ask) them to help him find out more about a painting he had. Robert's father ⁵____ (buy) a box of objects for £30 at an auction in 2003, which included a small painting. The painting ⁶____ (keep) in a drawer for many years and eventually it ⁷____ (give) to Robert.

After almost a year, Robert ⁸____ (tell) the truth about the painting on live TV. The experts ⁹____ (say) it was by the English artist, John Constable, and it was worth about £250,000! He was surprised, but very happy.

◂ Go back to page 80

129

GRAMMAR PRACTICE

10A Past perfect

We use the past perfect to describe an action that happened before another action in the past.

I arrived at the meeting late because I'd missed the train.
Justine hadn't studied for the exam so she failed it.
Had you met Sergio before you started the job?

We form the past perfect with *had* + the past participle of the main verb.

▶ 10.5	**Past perfect**
+	He**'d forgotten** his wallet so he couldn't buy anything.
–	We **hadn't tried** *ceviche* before we visited Peru.
?	**Had** you **trained** much before you ran the marathon?
Y/N	Yes, I **had**. / No, I **hadn't**.

Look! The contracted form of the past perfect is the same as the contracted form of *would*.
I'd seen him before. = *I had seen him before.*
I'd see him if I could. = *I would see him if I could.*

Narrative tenses

We usually use the past perfect with the past simple and the past continuous to show when actions happened.

When I got home, my husband made the dinner.

When I got home, my husband was making the dinner.

When I got home, my husband had made the dinner.

1 Match the halves to make sentences.
   1 Sofia had seen the film before _____
   2 Geoff felt very bad because _____
   3 Susana hadn't had lunch, so _____
   4 Paulo had grown a beard, so _____
   5 When I got to the station, _____
   6 Ali had finished the report when _____

   a I got to work this morning.
   b she felt very hungry.
   c and she said it wasn't very good.
   d the train had already left.
   e I didn't recognize him.
   f he'd forgotten his niece's birthday.

2 Complete the conversations with the past perfect form of the verbs in brackets.
   1 A Why did they walk to university today?
     B They _____ (have) a problem with the car.
   2 A _____ you _____ (hear) about the problems at the airport before you left?
     B No, I hadn't. Luckily, they _____ (not make) any changes to my flight.
   3 A Rita bought me a book for my birthday, but I _____ (read) it before.
     B It's my fault. She bought it because I _____ (recommend) it to her.
   4 A Was Grandma pleased that the kids _____ (draw) a picture for her?
     B Yes, she was. They _____ (not do) one for her before.
   5 A _____ Ricky _____ (look) everywhere before he cancelled his credit card?
     B No, he _____ (not look) in his sports bag. He found it there this morning.

3 Complete the text with the past simple, past continuous or past perfect form of the verbs in brackets.

On 21 April 1980, Rosie Ruiz ¹_____ (cross) the finishing line of the Boston Marathon with a time of 2:31:56 – the fastest female time in Boston Marathon history. However, when she ²_____ (receive) the winner's medal, some judges ³_____ (become) suspicious because she ⁴_____ (not sweat) very much. Then, two students ⁵_____ (say) that they ⁶_____ (see) her join the race half a mile from the finishing line. Later, photographer Susan Morrow said she ⁷_____ (meet) Ruiz while she ⁸_____ (travel) on the subway in her running clothes at the time of the New York marathon, six months earlier. The judges ⁹_____ (discover) that Ruiz ¹⁰_____ (do) the same thing to win the Boston Marathon.

◀ Go back to page 85

10C Reported speech

When someone speaks, we call what they say 'direct speech'. When we talk about what they said afterwards, we call it 'reported speech'.

'I don't like the website.' ⇒ My boss said that he didn't like the website.
'We reserved a room.' ⇒ They told me that they had reserved a room.

We use the verbs *say* and *tell* to report speech. We use *tell* with a noun or a pronoun when we want to say who the person was speaking to. We can add *that* to reported speech sentences.

'I'm sorry.' ⇒ He said (that) he was sorry.
⇒ He told me (that) he was sorry.

The tense of the verb usually changes when we report speech.

Direct speech		Reported speech
present simple	⇒	past simple
present continuous	⇒	past continuous
past simple	⇒	past perfect
present perfect	⇒	past perfect
past perfect	⇒	past perfect
am/is/are going to	⇒	was/were going to
will	⇒	would
can	⇒	could

Look! We also change pronouns and possessive adjectives in reported speech.
'I sold my car to Lenny.' ⇒ He said that he'd sold his car to Lenny.
'We'll send you the letter.' ⇒ They said they'd send me the letter.

▶ 10.12

	Direct speech		Reported speech
present simple	'I drink too much coffee.'	⇒	She told me she drank too much coffee.
present continuous	'We're studying for the exam.'	⇒	They said they were studying for the exam.
past simple	'Karl didn't go to the shops.'	⇒	She said Karl hadn't gone to the shops.
present perfect	'I haven't been to Paris.'	⇒	He said he hadn't been to Paris.
past perfect	'We'd seen the film before.'	⇒	They said they'd seen the film before.
going to	'Michelle is going to drive home.'	⇒	He said Michelle was going to drive home.
will	'I'll open the letter.'	⇒	He told me he'd open the letter.
can	'Ruby can't swim.'	⇒	They told him Ruby couldn't swim.

1 Choose the correct words to complete the sentences.
  1 My teacher *said* / *told* me that my English was improving.
  2 The doctor *said* / *told* you had to stay in bed.
  3 Viktor *said* / *told* he had made a big mistake.
  4 Someone *said* / *told* us that you had started a blog.
  5 They *said* / *told* everyone they would win the game.
  6 The newsreader *said* / *told* that scientists had discovered a new planet.

2 Rewrite these sentences in reported speech.
  1 'I'll see you on Tuesday.'
    My mum told me _____.
  2 'It's not going to rain this week.'
    The weather forecaster said _____.
  3 'I've never eaten a curry.'
    Julieta said _____.
  4 'We saw your brother at the airport.'
    They told me _____.
  5 'I hadn't heard the news.'
    Bobby said _____.
  6 'I can't come to your wedding.'
    Ravi told me _____.
  7 'I'm waiting for a phone call.'
    My boss said _____.
  8 'I don't do much exercise.'
    Sandra said _____.

3 Write the direct speech for the reported sentences.

  1 Sheila and Harold said that they wanted to tell me their news.
    _____
  2 They told me that they'd been to Egypt on holiday.
    _____
  3 They said they'd been excited because they'd never been there before.
    _____
  4 Sheila said that she'd never ride a camel again.
    _____
  5 Harold told me he was going to go back next year.
    _____

◀ Go back to page 89

GRAMMAR PRACTICE

11A *-ing*/infinitive verb patterns

We often use two verbs together. The form of the second verb changes depending on the first verb.

I want to learn a new language.
I enjoy learning new languages.

After some verbs, we use the infinitive with *to*.

▶ 11.2	infinitive with *to*
decide	She decided to travel the world.
arrange	We've arranged to meet at the airport.
expect	I expect to have the results next week.
forget	Marcus forgot to buy any paper for the printer.
hope	He hopes to be here soon.
agree	They haven't agreed to decrease the price.
can afford	He can't afford to go on holiday.
manage	The driver managed to stop the train.
learn	I'm learning to speak Arabic.
offer	They offered to pay for the meal.
plan	We're planning to open a new office.
try	Meenah's trying to finish the project on time.
want	My sister wants to find a new job.
would like	I'd like to have a rest now.
promise	Saul promised to help me with the work.

After other verbs, we use the *-ing* form.

▶ 11.3	*-ing* form
imagine	Can you imagine living until you're 150?
feel like	I feel like staying in bed all day.
enjoy	My son enjoys visiting his grandparents.
fancy	We fancy eating out tonight.
suggest	They've suggested installing some new software.
spend (time)	I spend a lot of time travelling to work.
miss	She misses seeing her friends.
finish	Tony's finished building the wall.
hate	I hate being late.
keep	Jorge keeps making mistakes.
like	He doesn't like cooking dinner.
love	I love playing golf.
can't stand	Ramon can't stand staying in a tent.
mind	They don't mind getting up early.
look forward to	I'm looking forward to seeing you at the party.

> **Look!** After some verbs, we can use the infinitive with *to* or the *-ing* form, with no difference in meaning, e.g. *start* and *continue*.
> *It has started to rain.*   *It has started raining.*
> *He continued to study.*   *He continued studying.*

---

1   Choose the correct form of the verbs to complete the sentences.

1   Have you finished *to clean* / *cleaning* the kitchen?
2   Josh arranged *to meet* / *meeting* Natasha at the cinema.
3   She promised *to do* / *doing* her homework.
4   I don't mind *to wait* / *waiting* for you.
5   They agreed *to repair* / *repairing* my dishwasher.
6   You should learn *to use* / *using* the computer.
7   We didn't expect *to see* / *seeing* them again.
8   He spent the whole morning *to sunbathe* / *sunbathing*.
9   Our teacher keeps *to give* / *giving* us lots of homework.
10 She offered *to help* / *helping* me with my English.
11 David suggested *to cancel* / *cancelling* the meeting.
12 Don't forget *to bring* / *bringing* warm clothes.

2   Complete the conversation with the correct form of the verbs in brackets.

Julia   Felipe and I have decided [1]_____ (move) back to Brazil.

Sophie   Really? I thought you liked [2]_____ (live) in Britain.

Julia   Yes, but we miss [3]_____ (see) our families and we'd like [4]_____ (have) our own house. We could never afford [5]_____ (buy) a place in London.

Sophie   When are you planning [6]_____ (leave)?

Julia   Well, we don't want [7]_____ (wait) too long, so we expect [8]_____ (go) some time in the next couple of months. I've already managed [9]_____ (find) a job, and Felipe is hoping [10]_____ (get) one soon.

Sophie   It won't be the same here without you. Do you promise [11]_____ (keep) in touch?

Julia   Yes, of course. And if you and Dan feel like [12]_____ (come) to Brazil for a holiday, you'd be very welcome.

Sophie   That sounds great. Don't forget [13]_____ (give) me your email address before you go.

Julia   Don't worry, I won't. We're trying [14]_____ (organize) a party before we go, so that we can say goodbye to everyone properly. Do you fancy [15]_____ (come)?

Sophie   I hate [16]_____ (say) goodbye to people, but yes, I'd love to come!

◀ Go back to page 95

11C Articles

We use articles (*a*, *an* or *the*) before nouns. Sometimes we don't need to use an article.

▶ 11.14	articles
Indefinite article *a/an*	I have **a** pet dog and **a** pet cat.
Definite article *the*	**The** dog is much bigger than **the** cat.
No article	I love animals, especially dogs and cats.

We use the indefinite article *a/an*:

- to talk about a person or thing for the first time.
  I've got two children – a boy and a girl.
- to talk about a person's job.
  My sister's an engineer.
- in expressions of frequency or measurement.
  I see him once a week.
  The fish costs £10 a kilo.

We use the definite article *the*:

- if we have already mentioned the person or thing or we know which one is referred to.
  The boy is called Alex, and the girl is called Lucy.
- if there is only one of the thing.
  The sun is setting.
  I'll check on the internet.
- before some countries, especially if they have two words or are plural.
  I live in the UK, but my brother lives in the Philippines.
- for specific places in a town.
  I went to the bank / the cinema / the theatre.
- for musical instruments.
  She plays the guitar.
- for superlatives.
  He's the fastest runner in the world.

We don't use an article:

- to talk about things in general (plural and uncountable nouns).
  Dogs are my favourite animals.
  Pollution is a big problem today.
- for some places we visit regularly.
  I'm not going to work today.
  He's working at home.
  She had to go to hospital.
- for meals, days of the week, months and years.
  On Tuesday, I'm having lunch with Jack.
  August is the hottest month of the year.

1 Complete the sentences with *a/an*, *the* or – (no article).
  1 We usually go to ____ cinema once or twice ____ month.
  2 I bought ____ new car yesterday, but this morning ____ engine won't start.
  3 He's one of five brothers. ____ youngest brother is ____ doctor.
  4 She flew from ____ Venezuela to ____ USA.
  5 Are you really scared of ____ spiders?
  6 How long have you played ____ piano?
  7 Neil Armstrong was ____ first man on ____ moon.
  8 I hope you both find ____ happiness together.
  9 What did you have for ____ breakfast this morning?
  10 We have ____ dinner together three times ____ year.
  11 She got ____ home from ____ work and went straight to ____ bed.
  12 ____ Friday is ____ busiest day of ____ week for us.

2 Correct the mistakes or tick (✓) the sentences if they are already correct.
  1 Is she student? ☐
  2 I'm staying in bed this morning. ☐
  3 Why don't you ask her out for lunch? ☐
  4 Excuse me, where is museum? ☐
  5 It's lovely day today. ☐
  6 The life is hard sometimes. ☐
  7 The driver of our taxi was from Mexico. ☐
  8 I went to bank this morning. ☐
  9 My wife has never liked tomatoes. ☐
  10 It's best present I've ever had. ☐

3 Complete the text with *a/an*, *the* or – (no article).

Hexoskin is [1]____ Canadian company founded in [2]____ 2006. It wanted to create [3]____ clothes that could record [4]____ information about our bodies. That's why they developed [5]____ smart shirt which contains lots of sensors. [6]____ sensors collect data about the wearer's movements, heart rate and breathing and send it to [7]____ computer. Ariane Lavigne is [8]____ Olympic athlete who uses it, and she says [9]____ technology gives her [10]____ advantage over other snowboarders.

◀ Go back to page 99

133

GRAMMAR PRACTICE

12A Defining relative clauses

We use relative clauses to say which person, thing or place we are talking about.

He's the actor who was Sherlock Holmes on TV.
It's a machine which makes bread.
That's the restaurant where I used to work.

We use the relative pronouns *who* or *that* to talk about people.

The man who sits next to me at work was ill today.
I saw the woman that works in the post office in the park.

We use the relative pronouns *which* or *that* to talk about things.

There are companies which organize weddings for people.
Luigi enjoys films that make him laugh.

We use *where* to talk about places.

I want to visit the stadium where Manchester United play football.
Jorge works in the hospital where I was born.

▶ 12.2	defining relative clauses
To describe people	He's the teacher **who** taught me English. Did you see the children **that** were singing?
To describe things	That's the dog **which** bit me on the leg. I don't want a car **that** has a big engine.
To describe places	I'll meet you in the square **where** we met last time.

Look! *Who, which, that* and *where* refer to a person, thing or place that's already been mentioned, so we don't need to use another word again.
Snakes are the animals which ~~they~~ kill most people each year.
I'd prefer to see the doctor who ~~she~~ saw me last time.
Ronald went to the cinema where we saw the Star Wars film ~~there~~.

1 A Complete the sentences with *who, which* or *where*.

1 Did you get the email _____ I sent you yesterday?
2 This is the nightclub _____ Nicola met her boyfriend.
3 There's a meeting at 2.00 p.m. for all employees _____ work in the Sales Department.
4 The office _____ she spends most of her time is in Kuala Lumpur.
5 The person _____ started this company is now a millionaire.
6 My father-in-law doesn't like films _____ are too violent.

B In which sentences could you also use *that*?

2 Add the correct words: *who, which,* or *where*. Then match the halves to make sentences.

1 An umbrella is something ___which___ ___f___
2 A DJ is someone _____ ____
3 A hospital is a place _____ ____
4 A credit card is something _____ ____
5 An enemy is a person _____ ____
6 A passport is a document _____ ____
7 A department store is somewhere _____ ____
8 A selfie stick is something _____ ____
9 A single parent is someone _____ ____
10 A prison is a place _____ ____

a you go when you're ill.
b you use when you travel abroad.
c you use to take a photo of yourself.
d brings up a child without a partner.
e criminals are sent.
f ~~you use when it rains.~~
g plays music in a club or on the radio.
h you can buy lots of different things.
i someone hates.
j you use instead of cash to buy things.

3 Combine the pairs of sentences using *who, which, that* or *where*. Remember not to use words that aren't necessary.

1 That's the restaurant. We're going there tonight.
That's the restaurant where we're going tonight.
2 I know the man. He lives in that house.
_____
3 Did you enjoy the film? You watched it last night.
_____
4 They're the neighbours. They have lots of parties.
_____
5 We've booked a holiday in the hotel. We stayed there last summer.
_____
6 My sister-in-law works for a company. It develops apps.
_____

◀ Go back to page 103

12C Uses of the -ing form and the infinitive with to

We use the *-ing* form after prepositions. In the negative, *not* goes before the *-ing* form.

Thanks for inviting me to your wedding.
I'm bored of not going out.
He's worried about failing his exam.

We also use the *-ing* form as the subject or object of a sentence. The *-ing* form functions as a noun.

Keeping in touch is so easy these days.
Reading is a great way to improve your English.
Not drinking soft drinks has helped me to lose weight.
John doesn't enjoy reading.
I love dancing.

We use the infinitive with *to* after adjectives. In the negative, *not* goes before the *to*.

I'm amazed to hear that they're going out with each other.
She was disappointed to lose the match.
It's impossible not to laugh when you watch this film.

We also use the infinitive with *to* to say why we do something (to express the purpose).

I went shopping to buy a new pair of shoes.
She left the office to meet a friend.
They're saving all of their money to get married.

Look! We use *for* + *-ing* form to explain the function of things, but we use the infinitive with *to* to explain the purpose of actions.
Function: *This button is for turning up the volume.*
Purpose: *You press this button to turn up the volume.*

12.6 -ing form/infinitive with to

After prepositions	I'm interested **in buying** a new laptop.
As subject/object of a sentence	**Cycling** is a great way to keep fit. I love **cycling**.
After adjectives	It's **easy to forget** he's only eighteen.
To express a purpose	We have to leave soon **to get there on time**.

GRAMMAR PRACTICE

1 Choose the correct words to complete the sentences.
1 Before *to say / saying* anything, please just listen to me.
2 She wants a better job *to earn / for earning* more money.
3 He's afraid of *to disappoint / disappointing* his father.
4 *To share / Sharing* photos is easy with Instagram.
5 I'm really sorry for *to miss / missing* your party.
6 I'm delighted *to tell / telling* you that we're getting married.
7 *To speak / Speaking* another language is really useful in business.
8 She's pleased *not to work / not working* for that company.
9 He gave me the ring *to look after / looking after* for him.
10 We thought about *not to go / not going* to the wedding.

2 Write sentences in the present tense using the *-ing* form or infinitive with *to*.
1 Drink / too much coffee / not be / good for you
   Drinking too much coffee isn't good for you.
2 She really / enjoy / go to the cinema
   _____
3 It / not be / expensive / eat / here
   _____
4 She / not be / afraid of / make mistakes
   _____
5 Cook / with friends / be / a nice way to relax
   _____
6 We / delighted / hear your news
   _____
7 He / not be / very good at / keep in touch
   _____
8 I / go / to the gym / keep fit
   _____

3 Complete the text with the correct form of the verbs in the box.

be   work   study   get   act

¹_____ happily married for over 50 years isn't easy, but that's what Paul Newman and Joanne Woodward were. In 1950, Paul was working for his family's business, but he was more interested in ²_____ , so at the age of 25 he went to Yale University ³_____ Drama. He was lucky ⁴_____ a job as an actor in a play called *Picnic*, where he first met Joanne. After ⁵_____ together in the film *The long hot summer* a few years later, they got married. And the rest, as they say, is history.

◀ Go back to page 107

VOCABULARY PRACTICE

7A City features

1 ▶ 7.1 Match the words in the box with the pictures 1–14. Listen and check.

| apartment block   pedestrian crossing   street light   signpost   pavement   bike lane |
| fountain   tunnel   crossroads   bridge   bench   litter bin   statue   traffic lights |

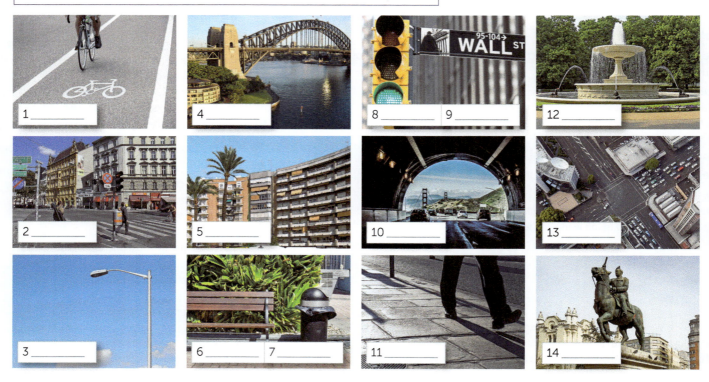

2 Choose the correct options to complete the sentences.
  1 The quickest way to the city centre is to go through the *bridge / tunnel*.
  2 He stopped because the *street lights / traffic lights* were red.
  3 Use the *pedestrian crossing / crossroads* – this road is dangerous.
  4 This area is really dirty. I think it's because there aren't any *benches / litter bins*.
  5 There's a big *statue / fountain* of a horse in the main square.
  6 Follow the *signposts / pavement* for the national museum.
  7 I don't like cycling here, there are no *apartment blocks / bike lanes*.
  8 Go along this street, and turn right at the *crossroads / litter bin*.

◀ Go back to page 58

7B Transport

1 ▶ 7.6 Match the words in the box with the definitions. Listen and check.

| car park   commuter   delayed   on time   parking space |
| passenger   platform   public transport   rush hour   traffic jam |

  1 The trains and buses people use to travel. _____
  2 The area in a station where you get on and off a train. _____
  3 A person travelling, but not driving. _____
  4 Someone who travels to work each day. _____
  5 An area or building where people leave their cars. _____
  6 The time of day when most people are travelling. _____
  7 A place where you can leave a single car. _____
  8 Slow or late. _____
  9 A long line of cars that move very slowly. _____
  10 Not early or late. _____

2 ▶ 7.7 Match the sentences. Listen and check.
  1 The trains never **arrive on time**. ____
  2 It **takes me** nearly two hours to get to work. ____
  3 Shall I **give you a lift** to the shops? ____
  4 I work at a local school, so I usually **go on foot**. ____
  5 I prefer to **ride my bike** into town. ____
  6 You need to **set off earlier**. ____
  7 It's much quicker to **go by taxi**. ____
  8 I have to **take a bus** and **a train** to work. ____

  a I'm going into town anyway.
  b That's why I always have my breakfast on the way.
  c You will find one outside the station.
  d I usually miss one of them!
  e Last week I waited nearly 50 minutes on the platform.
  f I always speak to people on the way.
  g You're always late for work!
  h It's faster than walking and there are good bike lanes.

◀ Go back to page 60

148

VOCABULARY PRACTICE

8A Food and drink

1 ▶ 8.1 Match the words in the box with the pictures 1–20. Listen and check.

| tomato sauce   beef   prawns   cereal   cucumber   salmon   lettuce   peppers   fruit juice   pineapple |
| strawberry   lamb   tuna   cabbage   coconut   turkey   flour   peach   aubergine   apple pie |

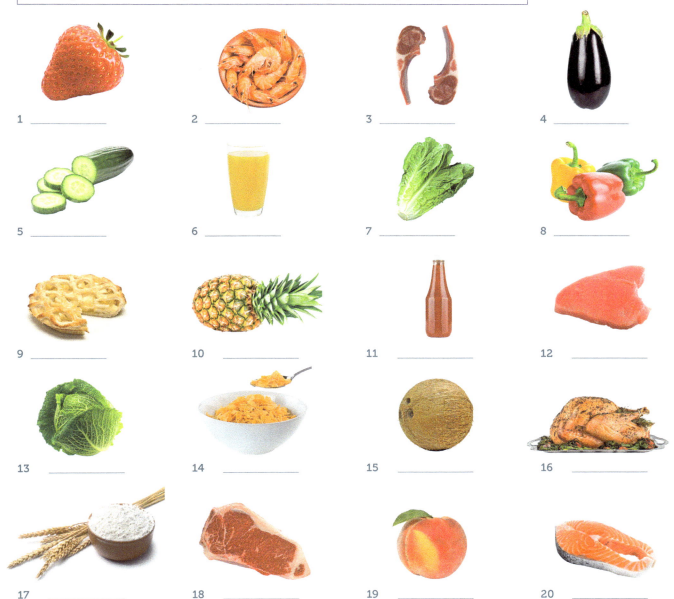

2 Complete the sentences with the words in the box.

| strawberries   tuna   cucumber   coconut   prawns   fruit juice   beef   lettuce   apple pie   tomato sauce   flour   cereal |

1 For breakfast, I usually have a bowl of _____ and a glass of _____.
2 It's easy to make bread. You just need _____, water and salt.
3 I'm allergic to seafood, I can't eat _____.
4 The simplest pizza only has _____ and cheese on the top.
5 It's difficult to open the shell of a _____, but the milk inside is delicious.
6 My grandmother is going to make an _____ for dessert tonight.
7 I'm going to make sushi tonight, so I need some rice and _____.
8 She always has a salad with tomatoes, _____ and _____ for lunch.
9 In the summer, I love eating _____ and cream!
10 I ate some amazing _____ steaks in Argentina.

◀ Go back to page 66

149

VOCABULARY PRACTICE

8C Adjectives to describe food

1 ▶ 8.8 Complete the descriptions 1–8 with the words in the box. Listen and check.

| spicy unhealthy tasty raw fresh crunchy salty delicious sour |
| disgusting healthy vegetarian bitter burnt creamy sweet |

1 You can't eat that _____ toast. It will taste _____ !

2 Sashimi is made with _____ fish. There's not much fat or salt, so it's very _____ .

3 I don't eat meat so I ordered a _____ curry, but it was so _____ I had to drink lots of water!

4 I know chips are _____ , but mmm! They're very _____ !

5 I don't like black coffee – it's too _____ . I prefer a _____ hot chocolate.

6 In Morocco, they make tea with _____ mint and lots of sugar, so it's very _____ .

7 You can't eat these snacks quietly – they're so _____ . They're _____ too, but perfect with a cold drink.

8 Oh no! I can't use this milk, it tastes a bit _____ . My cake has to be _____ to win the competition.

2 Choose the correct words to complete the sentences.

1 A Do you remember those *tacos* we ate in Mexico that were full of chilli peppers?
B I'll never forget that. They were so *burnt* / *spicy* / *crunchy* that I started crying!

2 A How often do you go to the supermarket?
B Hardly ever. I think the market is the best place to buy *fresh* / *raw* / *spicy* ingredients.

3 A Is something wrong with your cake?
B Yes, I used too much sugar and now it's too *salty* / *tasty* / *sweet*.

4 A What's *lassi*?
B Oh, you'll love it! It's a *disgusting* / *bitter* / *creamy* drink from India made with yoghurt.

5 A I have some lettuce, cucumbers and red peppers in the fridge.
B Great! Then we can make a nice *crunchy* / *creamy* / *salty* salad for lunch.

6 A Do you like lemon juice?
B No, I don't. It's too *spicy* / *sour* / *raw* for me.

◀ Go back to page 70

VOCABULARY PRACTICE

9A Money verbs

1 ▶ 9.3 Complete the sentences with the words in the box. Listen and check.

> owe   borrow   can afford   charge   cost   earn   get paid
> be worth   own   pay back   save   spend   waste   lend

1 Excuse me, how much does this necklace _____?
2 In my opinion, football clubs _____ too much for tickets.
3 Waiters can _____ a lot of money from tips.
4 Can you _____ me $50 until I get paid next week?
5 He has a rare 1950s Rolex watch. It must _____ a fortune!
6 As well as their flat in London, they _____ a house in France.
7 They _____ most of their money on clothes.
8 How much money do you _____ to the bank each month?
9 The car isn't ours yet. We still _____ £5,000 to the bank.
10 I've left all my money at home. Can I _____ £20, please?
11 Don't _____ your money on lottery tickets – you'll never win!
12 He's trying to _____ for an expensive holiday next summer.
13 She's so rich that she _____ to buy anything she wants.
14 We normally _____ on the last day of the month.

2 Choose the correct words to complete the sentences.

1 Oh no, I've forgotten my wallet. Can you *borrow / lend / owe* me some money?
2 I can't go out tonight. I don't *earn / afford / get paid* until next week.
3 Excuse me, how much does this jacket *cost / worth / charge*?
4 I *spend / waste / save* almost half of my money on rent every month.
5 If you give me $200, I'll *borrow / owe / pay back* the money next week.
6 I bought the guitar for $500, but it's now *worth / cost / earn* almost double that.
7 My car is very old, but I can't *spend / afford / own* to buy a new one at the moment.
8 When I finish university, I will *owe / lend / charge* more than $10,000 to the bank.
9 I shouldn't go out this month. I need to *charge / earn / save* for a new computer.
10 Why did you pay *back / waste / earn* all your money on these comics?

◀ Go back to page 77

9B Shopping

1 ▶ 9.5 Choose the correct verbs to complete the sentences. Listen and check.

1 Can I *pay by / pay with* credit card, or do I have to *pay by / pay with* cash?

2 I'd like to *exchange / return* this jacket – it's too big. Can I *exchange / return* it for a smaller one, please?

3 Can I *try on / fit* these shoes, please? I need to know if they *try on / fit* me.

4 You can *deliver / order* furniture online. Then the company will *deliver / order* it to your house.

2 ▶ 9.6 Match the words in the box with the definitions 1–12. Listen and check.

> changing room   bargain   receipt   discount   the sales   cash
> refund   till   window shopping   department store   queue
> shopping centre

1 A product which a shop sells at a very good price. _____
2 A piece of paper that shows you have bought something. _____
3 A time when a shop sells things for a lower price than usual. _____
4 The place in a shop where you can try on clothes. _____
5 A line of people that are waiting for something. _____
6 The place where you pay for things in a shop. _____
7 The money that is returned when a product isn't suitable. _____
8 An amount or percentage off the usual price. _____
9 Money in the form of notes and coins. _____
10 Looking at products in shops without buying anything. _____
11 A large shop with areas selling different types of products. _____
12 A covered area with different shops. _____

3 Match the halves to make sentences.

1 I'm going to try on these jeans ____
2 I'm sorry, I can't give you a refund ____
3 Please join the queue for this till, ____
4 This morning I went window shopping ____
5 I bought this handbag for £15 in the sales – ____
6 I bought it at the department store because ____
7 If I pay with cash, ____
8 I ordered these online last week, ____

a can you offer me a discount?
b in the changing room.
c but you can only pay by credit card.
d it was a real bargain!
e if there's a problem, I can return it easily.
f but I'd like to exchange them for a different colour.
g if you don't have the receipt.
h in the shopping centre.

◀ Go back to page 78

151

VOCABULARY PRACTICE

10A Sports and competitions

1 ▶ 10.2 Look at the football results. Complete the text with the verbs in the box in the correct form. Listen and check.

| win   beat   score   lose   draw |

On 28 May 2016, Real Madrid ¹_____ their rivals, Atlético, in the final of the UEFA Champions League. Ramos ²_____ a goal first, but 65 minutes later, Carrasco managed to score again to ³_____ 1–1. After extra time, Real Madrid were lucky to ⁴_____ the game on penalties. Atlético were very disappointed to ⁵_____ because in 2014, they had also lost to Real Madrid in the final.

Look! We use *win* for a competition or award, and we use *beat* for another team or opponent.
Real Madrid won the Champions League.
Real Madrid beat Atlético.

2 ▶ 10.3 Match the words in the box with the pictures 1–10. Listen and check.

| athlete   crowd   player   medal   race   referee
spectator   umpire   trophy   match |

3 ▶ 10.4 Read sentences. 1–4. Match the verbs in **bold** with definitions a–d. Listen and check.

1 Over 200 countries **take part** in the Olympic Games every four years. ____
2 It's difficult to **cheat** in sporting events, but some athletes still try. ____
3 Before you do any sport, you should always **warm up**. ____
4 I couldn't finish the marathon. I had to **give up** after 20 kilometres. ____

a break the rules to try to win a game or pass a test
b stop doing something because it's too difficult
c play in a game or competition
d do special exercises to prepare your body for sport

4 Choose the correct words to complete the sentences.

1 The *referee / umpire* showed three football players the red card.
2 I got injured because I didn't *give up / warm up* before the game.
3 My grandfather won a bronze *medal / race* in the Olympic Games.
4 The LA Lakers *beat / won* the Chicago Bulls by 123 to 118.
5 Serena Williams is a very successful *athlete / referee*.
6 Your team *cheated / scored*. This competition is for under 16s, but three of your players are 17 years old.
7 We *drew / lost* 0–0. It was a really boring game.
8 My sister was in the stadium, so when I watched the match on TV, I looked for her in the *crowd / spectator*.
9 The 100 metres *match / race* is my favourite part of the Olympics.
10 I'm terrible at tennis. I *beat / lost* my last match 0–6, 0–6, 0–6!

1 _____

2 _____

3 _____

4 _____

5 _____

6 _____

7 _____

8 _____

9 _____

10 _____

◀ Go back to page 84

VOCABULARY PRACTICE

10C Parts of the body

1 ▶ 10.9 Match parts of the body a–x with the words 1–24. Listen and check.

1 foot ____ 2 knee ____ 3 toes ____ 4 ankle ____

5 finger ____ 6 wrist ____ 7 elbow ____ 8 hand ____
9 arm ____ 10 thumb ____

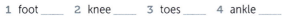

11 neck ____ 12 cheek ____ 13 chest ____ 14 lips ____
15 back ____ 16 chin ____ 17 forehead ____ 18 shoulder ____

19 heart ____ 20 brain ____ 21 stomach ____
22 skin ____ 23 muscle ____ 24 bone ____

2 ~~Cross out~~ the word that is incorrect in each sentence.

1 I got injured in a rugby match and now I can't move my *cheeks / elbow / shoulder*.
2 She can't walk because she's hurt her *ankle / brain / toes*.
3 I can't write because something is wrong with my *fingers / lips / wrist*.
4 It was so cold, she was wearing a scarf around her *elbow / neck / shoulders*.
5 This shirt doesn't fit me because I have quite a big *chin / neck / chest*.
6 It's impossible for me to run a marathon because of my bad *ankle / fingers / knee*.
7 Put this cream on your *lips / muscles / bones* if they hurt.
8 You need to have a scan at the hospital to see your *bones / heart / forehead* properly.
9 In a warm-up, you need to stretch your *chin / arms / muscles*.

◀ Go back to page 88

153

VOCABULARY PRACTICE

11A Household objects

1 ▶ 11.1 Match the words in the box with the pictures 1–20. Listen and check.

oven   sink   blanket   cushion   dishwasher   bin   duvet   pillow   fridge-freezer   iron   rug   sheets   wash basin   tap   air conditioning   washing machine   carpet   chest of drawers   central heating   wardrobe

1 _____

2 _____

3 _____

4 _____

5 _____

6 _____

7 _____

8 _____

9 _____

10 _____

11 _____

12 _____

13 _____

14 _____

15 _____

16 _____

17 _____

18 _____

19 _____

20 _____

2 Choose the correct word to complete the sentences.
1 Can you put these glasses in the *wash basin / sink*, please? They're dirty.
2 We need new *pillows / cushions* for the sofa. What colour shall we have?
3 Let's move the *rug / carpet* to the middle of the room.
4 Could you turn on the *air-conditioning / central heating*? It's cold in here.
5 We have a new *dishwasher / washing machine*. My shirts are so clean these days!
6 Help me make the bed. Can you pass the *sheet / blanket* to put on top?

◀ Go back to page 94

VOCABULARY PRACTICE

11B Housework

1 ▶ 11.6 Match the words in the box with the pictures 1–15. Listen and check.

| mop the floor   clear the table   lay the table   water the plants   load the dishwasher   do the ironing   vacuum the carpet   do the washing up
sweep the floor   take out the rubbish   make the bed   dust the furniture   hang out the clothes   do the washing   put away the toys |
|---|

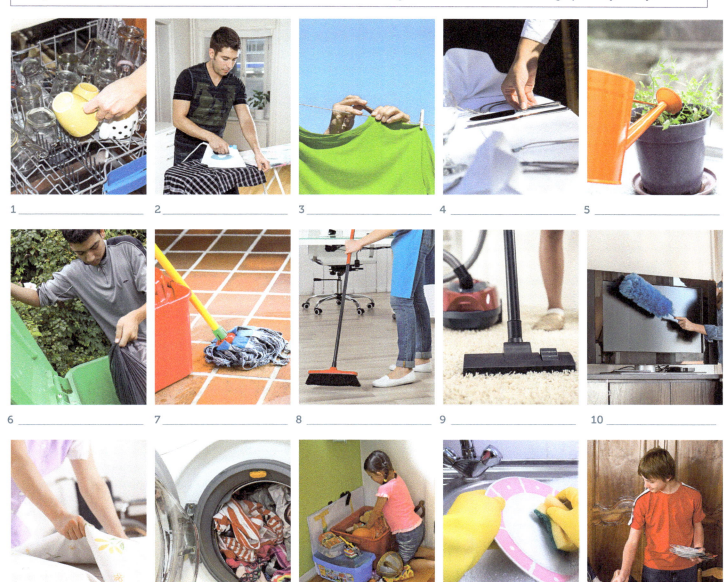

2 Choose the correct word to complete the sentences.

1 The first thing I do every morning is *lay / make / change* my bed.
2 You have to *do the washing up / do the washing / hang out the clothes*. The dishwasher is broken.
3 I have lots of allergies, so if I don't *clear / do / dust* the house every day, I start to sneeze and cough.
4 These plants will die if you don't *wash / water / clear* them more often.
5 Can you *hang out / take out / water* the clothes, please. They're very wet.
6 My dog leaves hairs on the rug, so I have to *vacuum / mop / clear* it every day.
7 What a wonderful meal! Can you help me *mop / clear / lay* the table?
8 My friends are coming to dinner in twenty minutes so I need to *clear / make / lay* the table.

◀ Go back to page 96

155

VOCABULARY PRACTICE

11C Words to describe materials and clothes

1 ▶ 11.12 Complete the descriptions 1–10 with the words in the box. You will need to use some of the words more than once. Listen and check.

denim cotton plastic leather silk fur wood/wooden glass wool/woollen metal

1 A _____ shirt. It's made of _____ .
2 A _____ coat. It's made of _____ .
3 Some _____ boots. They're made of _____ .
4 A _____ tie. It's made of _____ .
5 Some _____ shoes. They're made of _____ .
6 A _____ jumper. It's made of _____ .
7 A _____ necklace. It's made of _____ .
8 Some _____ jeans. They're made of _____ .
9 A _____ ring. It's made of _____ .
10 Some _____ beads. They're made of _____ .

2 ▶ 11.13 Match the adjectives with their opposites. Listen and check.
1 plain ____   a old-fashioned
2 smart ____   b loose
3 stylish ____ c patterned
4 tight ____   d casual

3 Look at the pictures. Are the sentences true (T) or false (F)? Correct the false sentences.

1 Helen is wearing a smart jacket. ____
2 She's wearing a silk scarf. ____
3 She's wearing tight trousers. ____
4 Joe is wearing casual clothes. ____
5 He's wearing a patterned jacket. ____
6 He's wearing a plain tie. ____
7 He has a wooden tennis racket. ____
8 He's wearing loose shorts. ____
9 He's wearing a plain T-shirt. ____

◀ Go back to page 98

VOCABULARY PRACTICE

12A Relationships

1 ▶ 12.1 Put the words in the box in the correct columns. Listen and check.

| cousin | only child | flatmate | employer | enemy | stranger | twin | ex-husband | stepsister | bride | colleague | neighbour |
| parents-in-law | boss | girlfriend | groom | single parent | relative | employee | business partner | classmate | brother-in-law |

family	couple	work/study	home	other

2 Complete the sentences with the words from exercise 1.
1 Daisy and I work in the same office. She's my _____ .
2 I'm an _____ . I don't have any brothers or sisters.
3 Harry and Luke share an apartment. They're _____ .
4 Carolina got divorced in 2013, but she still sees her _____ .
5 It was a lovely wedding. The _____ wore a long white dress, and the _____ wore a grey suit.
6 Our next-door _____ has just sold his house.
7 He's very friendly. He doesn't have an _____ in the world.
8 Her husband died, so she's a _____ to Emma, her daughter.
9 This is my _____ . We're not identical, but we look quite similar.
10 It's so friendly here. A _____ helped me when I was lost.

◀ Go back to page 102

12C Relationship verbs

1 ▶ 12.5 Complete the sentences with the past simple form of the phrases in the box. Listen and check.

| keep in touch | go out (together) | get back together | ask (someone) out | fall in love | get on (well/badly) |
| have (something) in common | become friends | get married | introduce | get to know | go on a date | break up |

Couple get back together after 30 years

Hannah Mason from the UK and Gustavo Ramos from Argentina first met in 1985. They were both travelling in France after finishing university. A friend ¹_____ Gustavo to Hannah, and they immediately ²_____ well. As they ³_____ each other better, they ⁴_____ good _____ . They discovered that they ⁵_____ a lot in _____ , including a love of travel.

Friendship turned to romance when Gustavo ⁶_____ Hannah _____ . They ⁷_____ to Gustavo's favourite restaurant in Paris, and before long they ⁸_____ in _____ . They ⁹_____ together for the rest of the summer, but they ¹⁰_____ when Hannah returned to the UK and Gustavo went home to Argentina.

They didn't ¹¹_____ , and that could have been the end of the story. But, 30 years later, Gustavo moved to the UK and contacted Hannah. They realized they still cared for each other, so it wasn't long before they ¹²_____ . And their story ended happily when they ¹³_____ last year.

2 Choose the correct words to complete the sentences.
1 We don't *have / make / do* a lot in common – in fact, we're completely different!
2 I think I'm falling *on / in / for* love.
3 Are Charlie and Sarah really *leaving / going / getting* out together?
4 They're getting *marry / marriage / married* next year.
5 Do you get *on / in / out* well with your brother?
6 It was my boss who introduced me *with / for / to* my future wife.
7 The first date that we went *to / in / on* together was to a rock concert.
8 They had a big argument and decided to break *up / off / out*.
9 We were classmates, but we only *became / got / came* friends after we left school.
10 I first *became / arrived / got* to know her when we worked together in Istanbul.
11 Has Sam ever asked you *out / up / off* for dinner?
12 James and I are thinking of *going / getting / joining* back together.
13 You must *go / have / keep* in touch while you're away.

◀ Go back to page 106

157

COMMUNICATION PRACTICE

7A Student A

1 Student B has recently moved to an apartment in another country. Find out if he/she has done these things.

  A *Have you unpacked your things yet?*
  B *Yes I have. The apartment looks great.*

  1 unpack your things
  2 set up the Wi-Fi
  3 meet your neighbours
  4 explore the local area
  5 register with a doctor
  6 open a bank account

2 You are going to London on holiday tomorrow. Look at your 'to-do' list and answer Student B's questions.

Things to do
find my passport ✓ (five minutes ago – in my desk)
pack the suitcase ✗
book a hotel ✓ (Astoria Hotel, Kensington)
buy some sun cream ✓ (went to shops an hour ago)
ask friend to look after pet ✗
decide what to do in London ✓ (city tour & shopping)

7C Student A

1 Complete the sentences with the present perfect form of the verbs in the box and *for* or *since*. Guess the correct options and tell Student B. He/She will tell you if you are correct.

| have collect be exist |

HOLLYWOOD FACTS

1 The Oscars award ceremony _____ _____ _____ 1929.
  The winner of the Best Actor award that year was *an American / a German / a Russian* actor, Emil Jannings.
2 The actor Johnny Depp _____ _____ *Barbie dolls / teddy bears / toy cars* _____ his daughter was little.
3 Hollywood actress Christina Ricci _____ _____ afraid of *plants / spiders / flying* _____ most of her life.
4 The actress Angelina Jolie _____ _____ *Chinese lessons / a pilot's licence / a pet snake* _____ more than ten years.

2 Listen to Student B's sentences and tell him/her if they are correct.

  1 There has been a big Hollywood sign in Los Angeles since 1923, but the first sign said 'Hollywoodland'.
  2 *Spiderman* actor Tobey Maguire and Leonardo DiCaprio have known each other since they were children.
  3 Actress Mila Kunis has played video games for many years.
  4 Eva Marie Saint, who won an Oscar for *On the Waterfront* in 1954, has lived in Hollywood for over 60 years and still works as an actress.

8A Student A

1 You are going to cook a big lunch for a group of friends. Student B will tell you what ingredients he/she has. Look at the list of ingredients and use the phrases in the box to help you reply.

| Great – that's enough.   That's too much.   That's too many.
  That's not enough.   We (only) need … |

2 You are going to cook a big lunch for a group of friends. Tell Student B what ingredients you have. He/She will tell you if you need more, less or if it is enough.

I have 500 grams of prawns.

INGREDIENTS
4 tins of tomatoes
1.5 kg of beef
2 red peppers
3 onions
1 pineapple
600g of strawberries
2 cartons of vanilla ice cream
2 litres of orange juice

COMMUNICATION PRACTICE

8C Student A

1 You and Student B are starting work as cooks in a school canteen. Guess the missing words. Student B will tell you if you are correct.

SCHOOL KITCHEN GOLDEN RULES!

HYGIENE

1 You have to wear _____ at all times, but you don't have to <u>wear gloves</u>.

2 You mustn't wear _____ in the kitchen.

3 You must wash <u>your hands</u> before you start work.

COOKING

4 You must use _____ in all the dishes and you mustn't use <u>too much salt or sugar</u>.

5 You must wash all _____ , but you don't have to wash <u>meat</u>.

6 You have to throw away _____ in the black bins.

MENU

7 You have to prepare <u>one vegetarian dish every day</u>.

8 You don't have to serve _____ on Fridays.

9 On Thursdays, you have to make <u>a curry</u>, but you mustn't make the sauce _____ .

10 On Wednesdays, you have to make <u>a Chinese dish</u>, but you mustn't make _____ .

8D Student A

1 Invite Student B to one of the events below. If he/she refuses, try another one.

Die Meistersinger von Nürnberg Fri 6.00 p.m.
Over four hours of German opera at the National Theatre

Pencils through the ages Sat 11.00 a.m.
A talk about the history of pencils at the City Museum

Local chess competition Mon 1.00 p.m.
32 local players compete to win the tournament

Karaoke night Tue 7.00 p.m.
Sing your favourite songs all night

2 Student B is going to invite you to some events. Refuse as politely as possible every time.

9A Student A

1 Complete the quiz questions with *used to* and the verbs in brackets.

Before they were famous

1 The singer, Madonna, _____ (work) in a doughnut shop. **True** or False?

2 The actor, Brad Pitt, _____ (dress up) as a chicken to advertise a fast-food restaurant. **True** or False?

3 The founder of Microsoft, Bill Gates, _____ (sell) hot dogs at his local baseball stadium. True or **False**? (He used to work as a computer programmer.)

4 The actor, Johnny Depp, _____ (feed) the penguins at a zoo in Kentucky. True or **False?** (He used to sell pens.)

5 The actor and comedian, Jim Carrey, _____ (live) with his family in a VW camper van. **True** or False?

6 The hip hop artist, Kanye West, _____ (work) as a shop assistant in GAP. **True** or False?

7 The actor, Tom Cruise, _____ (work) as a chef in a Chinese restaurant. True or **False?** (He used to work in a hotel, carrying luggage for guests.)

8 The actress, Julia Roberts, and former US president, Barack Obama, _____ (sell) ice cream. **True** or False?

2 Take it in turns to read your quiz questions to your partner. The correct answers are in **bold**.

9C Student A

1 Complete sentences 1–6 with the passive form of the verbs in brackets.

1 Which famous item of clothing _____ by Dorothy in the film *The Wizard of Oz?* (wear)
a A pair of blue boots b A green hat c **A pair of red shoes**

2 When _____ the first *Superman* comic _____? (publish)
a In 1901 b **In 1938** c In 1959

3 In 2015, some drums that belonged to Ringo Starr from The Beatles were sold at auction. How much _____ they _____ for? (sell)
a **$1.75m** b $5.5m c $800,000

4 Who _____ the picture *Guernica* _____ by? (paint)
a Andy Warhol b Salvador Dalí c **Pablo Picasso**

5 Who _____ the film *Star Wars: The Force Awakens* _____ by? (direct)
a Steven Spielberg b **J.J. Abrams** c George Lucas

6 Who _____ the songs 'Umbrella' and 'Diamonds' _____ by? (sing)
a Beyoncé b **Rihanna** c Lady Gaga

2 **A** Read your questions and the three possible answers to Student B. He/She must try to answer. The correct answers are in **bold**.

B Try to answer Student B's questions.

163

COMMUNICATION PRACTICE

10A Student A

1 A Guess the past perfect verbs to complete the sentences.

Kevin's flatmates were really angry with him because …
1 he _____ all the food in the fridge.
2 he _____ to the supermarket.
3 he _____ the dirty dinner plates.
4 he _____ all the milk.
5 he _____ the kitchen.

B Read your sentences to Student B. He/She will tell you if you are correct.

2 Listen to Student B's sentences. Tell him/her if they are correct or not.

Last night, Miriam's friends organized a party for her. She was really surprised because …
1 nobody had told her about it.
2 she hadn't seen some of her friends for years!
3 everyone had bought her a present.
4 she thought her friends had forgotten about her birthday.
5 all her friends had shouted "surprise!" when she came in.

10C Student A

1 You're a journalist. You interviewed Student B last week and made notes. Check the information with him/her and correct any mistakes.

A *Did you say that you were originally from South Africa?*
B *No, I told you that I was originally from Kenya.*

> Student B
> is originally from ~~South Africa~~ Kenya.
> has lived in Argentina for ten years.
> is married and has two children.
> can't speak Spanish.
> is going to the USA next week.
> studied dance in the Netherlands.

2 Student B is a journalist who interviewed you last week. Correct what he/she says using the information.

B *Did you tell me that you were Irish?*
A *No, I said that I was Scottish.*

> You're Scottish.
> You moved to Kyoto in 2010.
> You're learning to speak Japanese.
> You've been to China twice.
> You're going to take part in a marathon.
> You won't go to the Olympics next year.

10D Student A

1 You are a passenger at an airport. Follow the diagram and use the phrases in the box to have a conversation with the information desk assistant.

> Excuse me, I was hoping you could help me …   I'd also like to ask about …   Just one more thing.   Can I double-check?
> Could you give me some information about … , please?   Could I speak to someone about … ?

Passenger (Student A)	Information desk assistant (Student B)
Ask if there's a delay on the 2.00 p.m. flight to Madrid. →	Apologize and explain that there is a 30-minute delay on this flight.
Ask which gate the flight is leaving from and how to get there. ←	Say that the flight leaves from gate A22. Offer to print an airport map. Check the guest is satisfied.
Ask about a shop which sells newspapers and magazines. →	Explain that there are lots of shops, but suggest one on the third floor which has lots of foreign language newspapers.
Thank the assistant. →	Respond politely.

2 You are a receptionist in a hotel. Respond to Student B in a helpful way. Make offers and suggestions and check that he/she is satisfied.

Guest (Student B)	Receptionist (Student B)
Ask about the best way to get to the train station. →	Greet the guest and explain that the quickest way is to take a taxi. Offer to call a taxi for the guest.
Thank the receptionist. Say that you need to be at the station at 4.00 p.m. ←	Check the guest is satisfied.
Ask the receptionist about a good place to have lunch. ←	Recommend a restaurant on Queen Street. Give the guest a map and explain how to get there.
Thank the receptionist. →	

COMMUNICATION PRACTICE

11C Student A

1 A Complete the questions with the correct article: *a*, *an*, *the* or – (no article).

1 Is ____ stress ____ big problem for you and your friends?
2 What's ____ best way to get ____ good job?
3 Have you ever been to ____ USA or ____ Canada?

4 What did you have for ____ dinner ____ last night?
5 Would you like to have ____ English lessons on ____ internet?
6 When was ____ last time you went to ____ cinema?

B Ask Student B the questions and listen to his/her answers.

12A Student A

1 Ask and answer questions with Student B to complete the crossword. Use the phrases in the box to make definitions with relative clauses.

B *What's 3 down?*
A *It's someone who is the leader of a country.*

> It's someone who/that ... It's a place where ...
> It's something which/that ...

12C Student A

1 Answer Student B's questions. Use the table below. Tell him/her where you went and what you did.

B *What did you do yesterday?*
A *First, I went to the bank to take out some money.*
B *What did you do after that?*

Where	Why
the bank	take out some money
the shops	buy a new coat
the doctor	get the results of some tests
the market	get some fish
a café	meet some friends
the airport	pick up a friend from the USA

2 Ask Student B questions about what he/she did yesterday. Write down his/her answers in the table below.

A *What did you do yesterday?*
B *First, I went to the sports centre to have a swim.*
A *What did you do after that?*

Where	Why
the sports centre	to have a swim
the office	
the garage	
the hospital	
the hairdresser's	
the cinema	

12D Student A

1 Thank, congratulate or compliment Student B using phrases 1–5. Listen to his/her responses.

1 Wow, what a great presentation!
2 Your English is really good.
3 Thank you for dinner. It was delicious.
4 You found my wallet. Thanks a million!
5 Thanks so much for your help with the report.

2 Listen to Student B's thanks, congratulations or compliments. Respond using the phrases in the box.

> Thanks, it's just a second-hand one though.
> It was a pleasure. They're lots of fun.
> Thanks. Yours is really nice too, actually!
> Oh, it's just something I did when I was at college.
> It wasn't just me. We're a team.

165

COMMUNICATION PRACTICE

7A Student B

1 You have recently moved to an apartment in another country. Look at your 'to-do' list and answer Student A's questions.

Things to do
- meet your neighbours ✓ (they're very nice)
- open a bank account ✗
- explore the local area ✓ (got back 15 minutes ago)
- unpack your things ✓ (the apartment looks great!)
- set up the Wi-Fi ✗
- register with a doctor ✓ (went this morning)

2 Student A is going to London on holiday tomorrow. Find out if he/she has done these things.

B *Have you bought some sun cream yet?*
A *Yes. I went to the shops an hour ago.*

1 buy some sun cream
2 decide what to do in London
3 book a hotel
4 find your passport
5 ask a friend to look after your pet
6 pack your suitcase

7C Student B

1 Listen to Student A's sentences and tell him/her if they are correct.

1 The Oscars award ceremony has existed since 1929. The winner of the Best Actor award that year was a German actor, Emil Jannings.
2 The actor Johnny Depp has collected Barbie dolls since his daughter was little.
3 Hollywood actress Christina Ricci has been afraid of plants for most of her life.
4 The actress Angelina Jolie has had a pilot's licence for more than ten years.

2 Complete the sentences with the present perfect form of the verbs in the box and *for* or *since*. Guess the correct options and tell Student A. He/She will tell you if you are correct.

know   play   be   live

HOLLYWOOD FACTS

1 There _____ _____ a big Hollywood sign in Los Angeles _____ *1923 / 1953 / 1973*, but the first sign said 'Hollywoodland'.
2 *Spiderman* actor Tobey Maguire and *Leonardo DiCaprio / Kanye West / Joaquin Phoenix* _____ each other _____ they were children.
3 Actress Mila Kunis _____ _____ *golf / video games / chess* _____ many years.
4 Eva Marie Saint, who won an Oscar for *On the Waterfront* in 1954, _____ _____ in Hollywood _____ over 60 years and still works as *a designer / an actress / a musician*.

8A Student B

1 You are going to cook a big lunch for a group of friends. Tell Student A what ingredients you have. He/She will tell you if you need more, less or if it is enough.

I have six tins of tomatoes.

2 You are going to cook a big lunch for a group of friends. Student A will tell you what ingredients he/she has. Look at the list of ingredients and use the phrases in the box to help you reply.

Great – that's enough.   That's too much.
That's too many.   That's not enough.
We (only) need …

INGREDIENTS
1 whole salmon
500g of prawns
1 lettuce
1 cucumber
250g butter
1 litre of milk
200g of flour
1 coconut

170

COMMUNICATION PRACTICE

8C Student B

1 You and Student A are starting work as cooks in a school canteen. Guess the missing words. Student A will tell you if you are correct.

SCHOOL KITCHEN GOLDEN RULES!

HYGIENE

1 You have to wear <u>a hat</u> at all times, but you don't have to wear _____ .

2 You mustn't wear <u>jewellery</u> in the kitchen.

3 You must wash _____ before you start work.

COOKING

4 You must use <u>fresh ingredients</u> in all the dishes and you mustn't use _____ .

5 You must wash all <u>raw fruit and vegetables</u>, but you don't have to wash _____ .

6 You have to throw away <u>all burnt food</u> in the black bins.

MENU

7 You have to prepare _____ every day.

8 You don't have to serve <u>salad</u> on Fridays.

9 On Thursdays, you have to make a _____ , but you mustn't make the sauce <u>too spicy</u>.

10 On Wednesdays, you have to make _____ , but you mustn't make <u>sweet-and-sour sauce</u>.

8D Student B

1 Student A is going to invite you to some events. Refuse as politely as possible every time.

2 Invite Student A to one of these events. If he/she refuses, try another one.

Black-and-white night Thur 6.00 p.m.
Enjoy three films from the 1930s at Roxy Cinema

Crazy burger buffet Fri 7.00 p.m.
Eat as many hamburgers as you want for $12

Ballroom dancing lessons Sat 11.00 a.m.
Learn how to dance the waltz and cha-cha-cha

Benches of the world Sat 5.00 p.m.
An exhibition of Michael Lamb's photographs of benches

9A Student B

1 Complete the quiz questions with *used to* and the verbs in brackets.

Before they were famous

1 The singer, Beyoncé, _____ (sweep up) hair in her mum's hairdressing salon. **True** or False?

2 The actress, Jennifer Aniston, _____ (clean) salmon in a fish factory. True or **False**? (She used to clean toilets.)

3 The Australian actor, Hugh Jackman, _____ (teach) PE at a school in England. **True** or False?

4 The actor, Tom Hanks, _____ (sell) popcorn and peanuts at his local cinema. **True** or False?

5 The singer, Lady Gaga, _____ (work) in a library. True or **False**? (She used to work in a Greek restaurant.)

6 The actor, Sylvester Stallone, _____ (clean) the lions' cages at Central Park Zoo in New York. **True** or False?

7 The Rolling Stones singer, Mick Jagger, _____ (catch) rats at a London theatre. True or **False**? (He used to work in a hospital.)

8 The Russian billionaire, Roman Abramovich, _____ (sell) plastic ducks in a market. **True** or False?

2 Take it in turns to read your quiz questions to your partner. The correct answers are in **bold**.

9C Student B

1 Complete sentences 1–6 with the passive form of the verbs in brackets.

1 What famous items of clothing _____ by Harrison Ford in the *Indiana Jones* films? (wear)
   a A hat and raincoat   b **A hat and leather jacket**   c A baseball jacket and cap

2 When _____ the first Sherlock Holmes story _____? (publish)
   a In 1810   b **In 1887**   c In 1935

3 In 2011, one of Marilyn Monroe's dresses was sold at auction. How much _____ it _____ for? (buy)
   a $1.3m   b $3.2m   c **$4.6m**

4 Who _____ the sunflower pictures _____ by? (paint)
   a **Vincent Van Gogh**   b Henri Matisse   c Salvador Dalí

5 What sort of car _____ by the mad scientist Doc Brown in the *Back to the Future* films? (drive)
   a A Lamborghini   b A Ferrari   c **A DeLorean**

6 Who _____ the films *Titanic* and *Avatar* _____ by? (direct)
   a **James Cameron**   b Steven Spielberg   c Ridley Scott

2 **A** Try to answer Student A's questions.

   B Read your questions and the three possible answers to Student A. He/She must try to answer. The correct answers are in **bold**.

171

COMMUNICATION PRACTICE

10A Student B

1 Listen to Student A's sentences. Tell him/her if they are correct or not.

Kevin's flatmates were really angry with him because …
1 he had eaten all the food in the fridge.
2 he hadn't been to the supermarket.
3 he hadn't washed the dirty dinner plates.
4 he had drunk all the milk.
5 he hadn't cleaned the kitchen.

2 A Guess the past perfect verbs to complete the sentences.
Last night, Miriam's friends organized a party for her. She was really surprised because …
1 nobody _____ her about it.
2 she _____ some of her friends for years!
3 everyone _____ her a present.
4 she thought her friends _____ about her birthday.
5 all her friends _____ "surprise!" when she came in.

B Read your sentences to Student A. He/She will tell you if you are correct.

10C Student B

1 Student A is a journalist who interviewed you last week. Correct what he/she says using the information.

A Did you say that you were originally from South Africa?
B No, I told you that I was originally from Kenya.

> You're originally from Kenya.
> You've lived in Argentina for eight years.
> You're married and have one child.
> You can speak Spanish fluently.
> You're going to the USA next week.
> You studied dance in Belgium.

2 You are a journalist. You interviewed Student A last week and made notes. Check the information with him/her and correct any mistakes.

B Did you tell me that you were Irish?
A No, I said that I was Scottish.

> Student A
> is ~~Irish~~ Scottish.
> moved to Tokyo in 2010.
> is learning to speak Japanese.
> hasn't been to China before.
> is going to take part in a 10 km race.
> will go to the Olympics next year if it's possible.

10D Student B

1 You work on an information desk in an airport. Respond to Student A in a helpful way. Make offers and suggestions and check that he/she is satisfied.

Passenger (Student A)	Information desk assistant (Student B)
Ask if there's a delay on the 2.00 p.m. flight to Madrid.	Apologize and explain that there's a 30-minute delay on this flight.
Ask which gate the flight is leaving from and how to get there.	Say that the flight leaves from gate A22. Offer to print an airport map. Check the guest is satisfied.
Ask about a shop which sells newspapers and magazines.	Explain that there are lots of shops, but suggest one on the third floor which has lots of foreign language newspapers.
Thank the assistant.	Respond politely.

2 You are a guest staying at a hotel. Follow the diagram and use the phrases in the box to have a conversation with the receptionist.

> Excuse me, I was hoping you could help me …   I'd also like to ask about …   Just one more thing.   Can I double-check?
> Could you give me some information about … , please?   Could I speak to someone about … ?

Guest (Student B)	Receptionist (Student A)
Ask about the best way to get to the train station.	Greet the guest and explain that the quickest way is to take a taxi. Offer to call a taxi for the guest.
Thank the receptionist. Say that you need to be at the station at 4.00 p.m.	Check the guest is satisfied.
Ask the receptionist about a good place to have lunch.	Recommend a restaurant on Queen Street. Give the guest a map and explain how to get there.
Thank the receptionist.	Respond politely.

11C Student B

1 A Complete the questions with the correct article: *a*, *an*, *the* or – (no article).

1. Do you have ____ pet? What's ____ pet's name?
2. How many times ____ year do you go to ____ dentist?
3. Do you like ____ reading? Are you reading ____ book at the moment?
4. What time do you normally go to ____ bed at ____ night?
5. What's ____ worst food you've ever had in ____ restaurant?
6. Do you know anyone who is ____ architect or ____ designer?

B Ask Student A the questions and listen to his/her answers.

12A Student B

1. Ask and answer questions with Student A to complete the crossword. Use the phrases in the box to make definitions with relative clauses.

   A *What's 3 across?*
   B *It's a place where you can play football or go for a walk.*

   > It's someone who/that …   It's a place where …
   > It's something which/that …

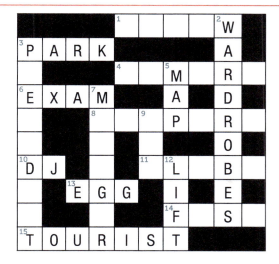

12C Student B

1. Ask Student A questions about what he/she did yesterday. Write down his/her answers in the table below.

   B *What did you do yesterday?*
   A *First, I went to the bank to take out some money.*
   B *What did you do after that?*

2. Answer Student A's questions. Use the table below. Tell him/her where you went and what you did.

   A *What did you do yesterday?*
   B *First, I went to the sports centre to have a swim.*
   A *What did you do after that?*

Where	Why
the bank	to take out some money
the shops	
the doctor	
the market	
a café	
the airport	

Where	Why
the sports centre	have a swim
the office	finish a report
the garage	get a light for my car
the hospital	visit my uncle
the hairdresser's	have my hair cut
the cinema	see the new *Batman* film

12D Student B

1. Listen to Student A's thanks, congratulations or compliments. Respond using the phrases in the box.

   > No problem. I enjoyed working on it!
   > It was no trouble at all. It was in my car.
   > Do you think so? I didn't have much time to practise.
   > Thanks, but I still need to improve.
   > Well, thank you for coming to visit us!

2. Thank, congratulate or compliment Student A using phrases 1–5. Listen to his/her responses.

   1. Did you paint this picture? It's fantastic.
   2. I'm very grateful for your help at this difficult time.
   3. I love your watch! It's cool.
   4. Thanks for looking after the children.
   5. Congratulations on your new car.

COMMUNICATION PRACTICE

11A Both students

1 In pairs, complete the sentences with the infinitive with *to* or the *–ing* form of the verbs in brackets.

Tell me about ...

1 something important you need _____ this week. (do)
2 a place you're planning _____ soon. (visit)
3 something you spend a lot of time _____ . (do)
4 a person you'd like _____ more often. (see)
5 something you can't afford _____ , but would love to have. (buy)
6 a household job you can't stand _____ . (do)
7 a film you're looking forward to _____ at the cinema. (see)
8 a mistake you keep _____ in English. (make)
9 a food you would miss _____ if you lived in another country. (eat)
10 someone you expect _____ later today. (see)

2 In pairs, take turns asking and answering the questions.

A *Tell me about something important you need to do this week.*
B *I need to buy a birthday card for my mum. What about you?*
A *I need to take my car to the garage.*

IRREGULAR VERBS

Infinitive	Past simple	Past participle
be	was, were	been
become	became	become
begin	began	begun
bite	bit	bitten
break	broke	broken
bring	brought	brought
build	built	built
buy	bought	bought
choose	chose	chosen
come	came	come
cost	cost	cost
do	did	done
dream	dreamt/dreamed	dreamt/dreamed
forbid	forbade	forbidden
forget	forgot	forgotten
forgive	forgave	forgiven
get	got	got
give	gave	given
go	went	gone, been
grow	grew	grown
have	had	had
hear	heard	heard
hide	hid	hidden
hold	held	held
keep	kept	kept
know	knew	known
learn	learnt/learned	learnt/learned
leave	left	left
let	let	let
lose	lost	lost

Infinitive	Past simple	Past participle
make	made	made
meet	met	met
pay	paid	paid
put	put	put
read (/riːd/)	read (/red/)	read (/red/)
ride	rode	ridden
ring	rang	rung
rise	rose	risen
run	ran	run
say	said	said
see	saw	seen
sell	sold	sold
send	sent	sent
sleep	slept	slept
speak	spoke	spoken
spend	spent	spent
stand	stood	stood
steal	stole	stolen
stick	stuck	stuck
swim	swam	swum
take	took	taken
teach	taught	taught
tell	told	told
think	thought	thought
throw	threw	thrown
understand	understood	understood
wake	woke	woken
wear	wore	worn
win	won	won
write	wrote	written

British English

Personal Best

Workbook **B1** Pre-intermediate

Richmond

UNIT 7 City living

GRAMMAR: Present perfect with *just*, *yet* and *already*

1 Order the words to make sentences. There may be more than one correct answer.

1 the / for / already / I've / tickets / paid
   _____.

2 you / have / finished / essay / yet / your
   _____?

3 it's / I've / 7 a.m. and / the house / cleaned / already
   _____.

4 just / spoken / the phone / I've / to Carolina on
   _____.

5 dinner / you / had / have / your / yet
   _____?

6 got home / I've / from work and / I'm tired / just
   _____.

7 already / done it / need to / you don't / go shopping / because I've
   _____.

8 you / Pedro's girlfriend / yet / met / have
   _____?

2 Complete the sentences with the verbs in the box. Use the present perfect and the words in brackets. There is one verb you don't need.

| eat   not open   spend   not make |
| come   cycle   take |

1 The bread's still warm. I _____ it out of the oven. (just)

2 I was going to have some chocolate, but you _____ it. (already)

3 Camila _____ any friends at her new school _____. (yet)

4 I gave both children €20 and they _____ it _____. (already)

5 I'm hot and sweaty because I _____ eight kilometres. (just)

6 They've built the new sports stadium, but they _____ it _____. (yet)

VOCABULARY: City features

3 Are the following sentences true (T) or false (F)?

1 You usually find bridges under the ground. ____
2 You can make statues from stone. ____
3 Traffic lights control the movement of cars. ____
4 Fountains send water into the air. ____
5 Apartment blocks are always low buildings. ____
6 At a crossroads, one road meets another. ____

4 Complete the words.

1 In towns and cities, it's safer to walk on the p___ ___ ___ ___ ___ ___ ___.

2 You can use a p___ ___ ___ ___ ___ ___ ___ ___ crossing to get across the road.

3 Is there a l___ ___ ___ ___ ___ b___ ___ that I can put this empty bottle in?

4 The road was very dark because there were no s___ ___ ___ ___ ___ l___ ___ ___ ___.

5 We drove through a long t___ ___ ___ ___ ___ under the river.

6 Let's sit on this b___ ___ ___ ___ to eat our sandwiches.

PRONUNCIATION: *just* and *yet*

5 ▶ 7.1 Listen to the sentences. Which sound do the underlined words start with? Write numbers 1–7 in the correct columns. Listen again and repeat.

/j/	/dʒ/
___ ___ ___ ___	___ ___ ___

1 Is Alfonso here <u>yet</u>?
2 Have you already been to the <u>gym</u>?
3 Anna's <u>just</u> left secondary school.
4 Vinicius <u>usually</u> has dinner with us on Friday.
5 He's applied for a new <u>job</u>.
6 Hi! How are <u>you</u>?
7 They look so <u>young</u>!

38

SKILLS 7B

LISTENING: Listening for facts and figures

1 Read the sentences from the audio about cycling. What type of information is missing? Match the gaps with a–f.

1 It's cheap, it's _____ and, more than anything, it's quick. ___
2 Of course, I love to walk, too, but if I go anywhere on foot, it _____ so long. ___
3 There are only about _____ people living here. ___
4 I can cycle from one end of town to the other in _____. ___
5 If I drive to work at _____ in the morning, it takes me half an hour. ___
6 If I cycle, I can get to the office at _____. ___
7 When I arrive somewhere, I don't have to find a _____. ___
8 All in all, I probably cycle for about _____ a week. ___

   a time
   b verb
   c noun
   d adjective
   e duration of time
   f number

2 ▶ 7.2 Listen and complete the gaps in exercise 1.

3 ▶ 7.3 Look at the example Listen to these sentences. Mark where the /t/ sound links with the next word and where it is not pronounced.

1 Matt and I have already walk(ed) ten miles!
2 We gave Bret a lift to the station.
3 She missed the bus so she went on the train instead.
4 I've just seen Anna and Scott in the car park.
5 He picked up his bag and crossed the road.

4 Order the letters to make words to complete the sentences.

1 He drove around the car park twice, trying to find a KRAGNIP CASPE _____.
2 We stood on the FLAMTROP _____, waiting for the train to arrive.
3 If we ETS FOF _____ at nine o'clock, we should arrive at midday.
4 I'm driving to Maria's house so I could give you a FILT _____.
5 I usually cycle there. It takes too long to go NO TOFO _____.
6 We were stuck in a RACFFIT MAJ _____ for almost an hour.
7 My favourite form of BUPCLI PARTNORTS _____ is the bus.
8 HURS HURO _____ starts just before seven every morning.
9 The train was full of MOCMETURS _____ on their way to work.
10 If we leave now, we should get there NO MEIT _____.

39

7C LANGUAGE

GRAMMAR: Present perfect with *for* and *since*

1 Complete the sentences with *for* or *since*.

1 We've known Murat _____ over ten years.
2 I've been a member of this gym _____ 2014.
3 My parents haven't heard from Beyza _____ March.
4 Have you seen Ahmet _____ you arrived?
5 I've been waiting here _____ ages!
6 Aline has been ill _____ over three weeks now.
7 I haven't driven _____ I passed my test.
8 They've lived in the same apartment _____ years.
9 Paolo hasn't eaten meat _____ he was a child.
10 Have you two known each other _____ a long time?

2 Complete the questions and answers.

1 A How many years was she a teacher?
   B She _____ a teacher _____ three years.
2 A How long were you in hospital?
   B I _____ there _____ two months.
3 A How long _____ Gabriela _____ a vegetarian?
   B Ten years.
4 A How many years _____ you and Paolo _____ married?
   B Nearly five.
5 A How long _____ your father in the army?
   B From 1990 till 2005.
6 A How long _____ you study medicine for?
   B I studied _____ eight years – until 2014.

3 Use the prompts to write questions and answers. Use the present perfect form of the verbs with *for* or *since*.

1 A how long/you/live/in Madrid
   _____?
   B I/be/here/three years
   _____.

2 A how long/she/be/asleep
   _____?
   B she/be/asleep/5.30
   _____.

3 A how long/Luis/have/a cough
   _____?
   B he/have/it/the weekend
   _____.

4 A how long/your cousins/work/in France
   _____?
   B they/work there/over ten months
   _____.

PRONUNCIATION: *for* and *since*

4 ▶ 7.4 Practise saying the sentences. Are *for* and *since* stressed (S) or unstressed (U)? Listen, check and repeat.

1 I've been here for three hours.   S   U
2 She's felt ill since Wednesday.   S   U
3 We've known about it since midday.   S   U
4 Livia has lived in Paris for six months. S   U
5 They haven't heard from her since April. S   U
6 I haven't eaten since breakfast.   S   U
7 We haven't seen Maria for years.   S   U
8 She's been away since 2014.   S   U

40

SKILLS 7D

WRITING: Writing an essay

1 Read Otto's essay and complete it with these linking words and phrases.

a The second reason   c Firstly
b In conclusion   d Finally

Should cars be banned from the city centre?

I live in a beautiful, historic city, but everyone agrees that there is a problem with traffic. Every day, over 60,000 people drive into the city centre for work or study, and pollution levels are rising. Our local council has suggested banning all cars from the city centre. Personally, I think this is a very bad idea.

1 _____, how would people get to work? Houses in the city are very expensive, and people who live outside the city already have long journeys to work. In my view, it is unreasonable that they should have to wait for a bus to travel into the city centre.

2 _____ is that I don't believe that it's possible for some people to use public transport or walk or cycle to work. For example, people in wheelchairs need special vehicles, and many people have to carry heavy tools or equipment for their work.

3 _____, I'm worried that local shops and businesses will suffer. If people can't drive to the shops, they won't come at all. Most people don't want to carry bags full of shopping on a bus.

4 _____, I feel that banning cars from the city centre is a bad idea. I would say that we should be looking at different ways of reducing pollution – ways that don't involve making life difficult for people! For example, we should develop better electric cars, improve public transport and make better cycle routes.

2 Find these phrases in Otto's essay. Then write sentences with your own ideas about whether or not cars should be banned from city centres.

1 Personally, _____.
2 In my view _____.
3 I don't believe that _____.
4 I'm worried that _____.
5 I would say that _____.

3 Use the words in the box to complete the arguments against Otto's opinion.

fresh air   pollution   healthier
public transport   permission   safe

1 In my opinion, banning cars would reduce _____.

2 I don't believe that it's _____ for cars and bicycles to share the road.

3 I think that getting some _____ by walking or cycling to work is a good idea.

4 People who need to carry heavy equipment could get _____ from the council to drive.

5 Personally, I feel that people who can't walk or cycle should use _____.

6 I wouldn't say that cycling is difficult for most people, and it makes them _____.

4 Write an essay giving the opposite opinion to Otto's.

- Use ideas from exercise 3 or your own ideas.
- Organize your ideas into five paragraphs: introduction, reasons 1–3, conclusion.
- Give examples or evidence to support your opinion.
- Use some of the phrases from exercise 2.

7 REVIEW and PRACTICE

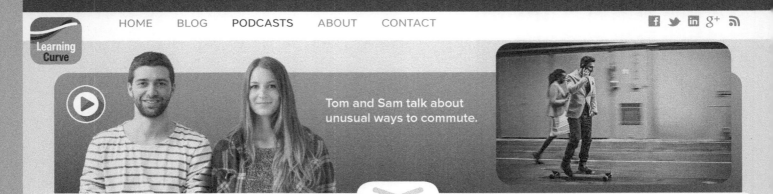

LISTENING

1 ▶ 7.5 Listen to the podcast. What does the speaker say is the main advantage of how he commutes?

a It's a healthy way to get to work.
b His journey is quicker than other people's.
c He can still wear a suit while he's travelling.

2 ▶ 7.5 Listen again. Complete the sentences with one or two words.

1 It takes Louie about _____ to get to work.
2 He rides his skateboard on the _____.
3 He has been skateboarding for _____ years.
4 He thinks other people are _____ of his journey to work.
5 He says the best thing about not using _____ is not waiting for buses.
6 He thinks skateboarding is less _____ than cycling.
7 He also uses his skateboard to go to _____.

READING

1 Read the blog about car-free cities. Match 1–4 with paragraphs A–D.

1 places where little is being done to reduce car use ____
2 how some cities have encouraged people not to drive ____
3 how technology can help people to manage without cars ____
4 a new city where people won't need to drive ____

2 Are the sentences true (T), false (F), or is there not enough information to decide (N)?

1 People often need to drive to other places on their way to and from work. ____
2 Most people who work in cities drive to work. ____
3 In Milan, most people travel by public transport once or twice a week. ____
4 London is a safe place to cycle to work. ____
5 In the new town near Chengdu, it will be easy for most people to walk everywhere. ____
6 Planners want people who work in Chengdu to drive there very quickly in their own cars. ____
7 It is easy for people in Helsinki to get information to help them travel without cars. ____
8 Most people in Helsinki already use public transport. ____
9 It is convenient for some people in US towns to cycle around their cities. ____
10 In Sydney, town planning makes it easy for people to use cars rather than public transport. ____

REVIEW and PRACTICE 7

HOME   BLOG   PODCASTS   ABOUT   CONTACT

Guest blogger Penny writes about how cities are designed.

Car-free cities – dream or reality?

What's the number one thing you hate about cities? It's probably the traffic. Who wants to breathe in dirty air all day, or spend hours stuck in a traffic jam on their daily commute? On the other hand, we've had cars for over 100 years now and we rely on them, especially with our busy lives – rushing to drop the kids off at school before we go to work, or going to the supermarket on the way home. So how can town planners persuade us to leave our cars at home? Here are some different ideas from around the world.

A Since 2014 Milan has had a really interesting system – for every day a resident leaves their car at home, they get a voucher for the value of a ticket on the train or bus! And in Copenhagen around half of all workers commute by bike on a huge, safe network of bike lanes. Perhaps London should try to do the same – traffic there moves more slowly than the average cyclist, but the streets are far more dangerous on two wheels!

B In some countries, town planners working on new towns and cities are trying to reduce car use to the minimum possible before they've even been built. For example, one new town in China, with a planned population of 80,000, is being designed so that all its shops, entertainment venues, work places, etc. are within a fifteen-minute walk of where residents live. And there'll be fast public transport connections to the nearest big city of Chengdu.

C In Helsinki, local authorities are using phone apps to reduce car numbers. The city has several schemes for people to share the use of bikes and cars. The app allows anyone to quickly find the nearest shared bike, car, or taxi, or tells them the best and fastest bus or train route. Planners there hope that within ten years no one will need to drive in the city at all.

D Sadly, not all cities are encouraging car-free journeys. It's true that 60% of people living in Paris don't own a car, but many US towns are designed specifically for car use, and there aren't any alternatives yet. And in car-loving Sydney, things seem to be going backwards – there are plans to get rid of pedestrian space to make room for even more cars!

UNIT 8 Food for thought

8A LANGUAGE

GRAMMAR: *Too, too many, too much* and *(not) enough*

1 Match the pairs of sentences.

1 She needs a holiday. ____
2 I can't wear this jumper on a warm day. ____
3 She felt uncomfortable after the meal. ____
4 Can you open the window? ____
5 Let's put the heating on. ____
6 This coat's no good for winter. ____
7 She won't pass the exam. ____
8 She was hungry when she went to bed. ____

a She works too hard.
b It's too hot in here.
c It's not thick enough.
d She doesn't work hard enough.
e She didn't eat enough.
f It isn't hot enough in here.
g It's too thick.
h She ate too much.

2 Complete the conversation with *too, too many, too much* or *(not) enough*.

A I'm so worried about my exams. I haven't done ¹_____ work.
B I feel the same! I think I'm doing ²_____ subjects. I work late every evening, but then I'm ³_____ tired to concentrate in class.
A I'm especially worried about French. Our teacher doesn't explain things clearly ⁴_____ and he doesn't give us ⁵_____ time to write things down.
B My problem is History. There's ⁶_____ information to write and there's ⁷_____ time. I want to study History at university, and if my exam results aren't good ⁸_____, I won't be able to.
A Well, try not to worry about it ⁹_____!
B You're right. Getting ¹⁰_____ stressed won't help!

VOCABULARY: Food and drink

3 Order the letters to complete the words.

1 s___ ___ ___ ___ ___   MONAL
2 a___ ___ ___ ___ ___ ___ ___   BIERNUGE
3 p___ ___ ___   CHAE
4 a___ ___ ___ p___ ___   EPPL EI
5 p___ ___ ___ ___   PPSREE
6 f___ ___ ___ j___ ___ ___ ___   TIUR CIUE
7 p___ ___ ___ ___ ___ ___ ___   EAINLEPP
8 t___ ___ ___ ___ s___ ___ ___ MOOTA UACE
9 c___ ___ ___ ___ ___ ___ ___   UUMCREB
10 t___ ___ ___   NAU

4 Complete the crossword. The first letters and total number of letters are given.

Across
4 meat from a sheep (4)
5 lots of people eat this for breakfast with milk (6)
8 a soft red fruit – you can make jam with it (10)
9 a fruit with a hard brown outside and a white part and liquid inside (7)
10 meat from a cow (4)

Down
1 a small, pink sea animal with a shell (5)
2 a vegetable with lots of green leaves; we usually cook it (7)
3 meat from a large bird (6)
6 a green salad vegetable (7)
7 we use this powder to make bread, cakes, etc. (5)

PRONUNCIATION: *too much sugar*

5 ▶ 8.1 Look at the underlined words. Listen and circle the vowel sound that you hear. Listen, check and repeat.

	/uː/	/ʌ/	/ʊ/
1 What <u>should</u> I do now?	/uː/	/ʌ/	/ʊ/
2 There aren't <u>enough</u> strawberries.	/uː/	/ʌ/	/ʊ/
3 I'm going to <u>cook</u> dinner.	/uː/	/ʌ/	/ʊ/
4 May I <u>use</u> your pen?	/uː/	/ʌ/	/ʊ/
5 Would you like a <u>cup</u> of coffee?	/uː/	/ʌ/	/ʊ/
6 I hate tomato <u>soup</u>!	/uː/	/ʌ/	/ʊ/
7 There wasn't any <u>food</u> left.	/uː/	/ʌ/	/ʊ/
8 Shall I <u>put</u> the heating on?	/uː/	/ʌ/	/ʊ/

44

SKILLS 8B

READING: Scanning for specific information

Food stories
ABOUT US   RECIPES   INGREDIENTS   SHOP

Aquafaba ('Aqua what?!')

As regular readers of this blog will know, I know my food! I always say, give me a dish from pretty much anywhere in the world and, within two minutes, I'll tell you what's in it. However, this weekend, I discovered that maybe I don't know quite as much as I thought I did. A vegan friend of mine invited me over for dinner. (He turned vegan five years ago after seeing a really shocking movie on the dairy industry.) Just to remind you, vegans avoid all animal products, including honey. So I was expecting beans to be on the menu (and they were – lots of them – in the main course). But it was the dessert that took me by surprise – vegan ice cream. And how do you make ice cream, I hear you ask, without milk, cream or eggs? (I should say, how do you make nice, creamy ice cream without dairy products, because I've had some fairly unpleasant vegan ice creams in my time!) Well, it turns out that the key to good vegan ice cream – and a whole load of other desserts – is bean water. Yes, you read that correctly – bean water, i.e. the water that beans have been boiled in. (You know, the stuff you usually throw down the sink.) Bean water, my friend tells me, is called 'aquafaba' by the vegan community. It's increasingly used to replace egg whites in savoury and sweet vegan dishes, such as vegan butter, cheese, biscuits and cakes. And I can honestly say it works, although it does give the ice cream a slightly odd smell. It's so good, in fact, that the morning after my dinner date, I went straight to the supermarket for a tin of beans. As I write, my first batch of aquafaba ice cream is firming up nicely in the freezer!

1 Underline the key words in these questions. Then scan the text about an unusual food and choose the best answer.

1 What did the blogger's friend invite her over for?
  a dessert
  b dinner
  c a dish containing eggs
2 What do vegans avoid eating?
  a milk and eggs
  b honey and cream
  c all animal products
3 What was the blogger expecting to be given to eat?
  a beans
  b vegan ice cream
  c a dessert
4 What, according to the blogger, is the key to many good vegan desserts?
  a beans
  b bean water
  c cream
5 In vegan cooking, aquafaba is used to replace
  a cream.
  b egg whites.
  c dairy products.

2 Look at the sentences. Write T for true sentences, F for false sentences, and N when the article doesn't give you enough information to be sure.

1 The blogger is a vegetarian, not a vegan. _____
2 The blogger's vegan friend has never eaten animal products. _____
3 The main course of the meal included beans. _____
4 This was the first time the blogger had eaten vegan ice cream. _____
5 The blogger says that aquafaba is usually thrown away. _____
6 Aquafaba is much healthier than egg white. _____
7 She says the smell of this vegan ice cream is especially nice. _____
8 She has now tried making vegan ice cream with aquafaba herself. _____

3 Choose the correct linkers to complete the sentences. There may be more than one correct answer.

1 I liked the vegan ice cream, *however / but / although* I found the idea of bean water a little strange at first.
2 *Although / However / But* I'd tried lots of vegan ice creams, I'd never especially enjoyed them.
3 I don't have a recipe for the ice cream, *however / although / but* I'm going to follow my friend's instructions.
4 I usually know what's in a dish. *But / Although / However*, I have no idea what's in this.
5 I don't usually cook vegan food. *However / Although / But*, I feel inspired to try now.

45

8C LANGUAGE

GRAMMAR: Must(n't) and (not) have to

1 Choose the correct options to complete the sentences.

1 You ___ finish that pie if you don't want it.
   a don't have to   b must   c mustn't
2 To pass this exam, you ___ score over 75%.
   a mustn't   b don't have to   c must
3 You ___ talk to Peter because he has a lot of work to do.
   a must   b don't have to   c mustn't
4 This is Ben's medicine. He ___ take it three times a day.
   a mustn't   b have to   c has to
5 Do we ___ bring our own food?
   a must   b don't have to   c have to
6 I have an important meeting. I ___ be late.
   a don't have to   b mustn't   c have to
7 My new job is close to my house, so I ___ catch the train.
   a mustn't   b don't have to   c have to
8 If you hear the fire alarm, you ___ leave the building immediately.
   a don't have to   b mustn't   c must
9 Why are you going home? Do you ___ get up early tomorrow?
   a have to   b must   c mustn't
10 It's Gina's birthday next week. I ___ forget to send her a card.
   a don't have to   b mustn't   c must

2 Complete the sentences with *must*, *mustn't*, or the correct form of *(not) have to*. There may be more than one correct answer.

1 We're going for a walk, but you _____ come if you're too tired.
2 There are thieves in the area, so you _____ make sure your car is locked.
3 Does Harry _____ wear his uniform on the school trip?
4 We _____ swim here – it's too dangerous.
5 Marta is very rich, so she _____ work.
6 Larry is in a hurry because he _____ catch a bus in five minutes.
7 Do the children's parents _____ sign these forms?
8 We can leave the classroom at any time. We _____ ask for permission.

VOCABULARY: Adjectives to describe food

3 Complete the sentences with the adjectives in the box.

| creamy | salty | sour | healthy | sweet |
| crunchy | bitter | delicious | | |

1 A _____ diet should include plenty of fresh vegetables and fruit.
2 Alex is such a good cook. He made an absolutely _____ curry last week.
3 You shouldn't eat too many _____ foods like crisps and olives.
4 Someone left the biscuits out all night and they're not _____ any more.
5 The coffee was much too strong and had a rather _____ flavour.
6 Mira loves _____ foods like chocolate and cakes.
7 She served the apple pie with a lovely _____ sauce.
8 Add sugar to the lemon juice, otherwise it will taste too _____.

4 Complete the adjectives.

1 Laura put a lot of chillies in the soup and it was too s___ ___ ___ ___.
2 Rob forgot to take the potatoes out of the oven and they were b___ ___ ___ ___ ___.
3 You haven't cooked this chicken long enough – it's still r___ ___ in the middle!
4 Paul loves un___ ___ ___ ___ ___ ___y foods like pizza and burgers.
5 You can make a t___ ___ ___y soup with chicken bones.
6 Does the restaurant use f___ ___ ___ ___ vegetables from their own garden?
7 Bean ice cream? It sounds d___ ___ ___ ___ ___ ___ing!
8 I don't eat meat – are there any v___ ___ ___ ___ ___ian dishes?

PRONUNCIATION: Sentence stress

5 ▶ 8.2 Practise saying the sentences, putting the main stress on the underlined modal verb. Listen, check and repeat.

1 You <u>must</u> bring your passport with you.
2 Do we <u>have</u> to leave tomorrow morning?
3 She <u>mustn't</u> take the hotel towels to the beach.
4 You don't <u>have</u> to wait if you don't want to.
5 Parents <u>mustn't</u> help their children with this homework.
6 She <u>has</u> to arrive there before 9 a.m.

SKILLS 8D

SPEAKING: Making and responding to invitations

1 ▶ 8.3 Listen to the conversation between Karl and Brigit. Complete the phrases.

1 Do _____ trying that new Japanese restaurant tonight?
2 I'm _____ I've already got _____.
3 But would you be _____ the Japanese place another evening?
4 OK then, do you _____ go on Saturday instead?
5 Oh _____, I think _____ that evening.
6 Yeah. That would be _____, except I'll have to leave quite early.
7 Would _____ to stay over at my place?
8 That's _____ of you, thanks.

2 Are phrases 1–8 in exercise 1 used for inviting (I), accepting (A) or refusing (R)?

1 ____
2 ____
3 ____
4 ____
5 ____
6 ____
7 ____
8 ____

3 ▶ 8.4 Listen to four people refusing invitations. Tick (✓) the things each speaker does.

	Speaker 1	Speaker 2	Speaker 3	Speaker 4
Use pleasant intonation				
Apologize before saying something negative				
Give explanations				

4 ▶ 8.5 Read the conversation then complete what B says. There is more than one possible answer for each gap. Then listen and say B's part aloud.

A Would you be interested in going to the cinema on Saturday? There's a new action movie that's meant to be really good.
B ¹_____. My parents are having a party. It's been planned for a long time and I can't miss it.
A Oh sure, I understand. The movie's on all week though. Do you fancy going another night?
B ²_____. I read an online review and it sounds really exciting. Sunday's good for me.
A Great. Would you like to come round to my place for a quick dinner before we go?
B ³_____. Why don't I bring something for dessert?
A Excellent! See you then. Bye for now.

47

8 REVIEW and PRACTICE

Tom and Sam talk about healthy eating.

LISTENING

1 ▶ 8.6 Listen to the podcast. Choose the best summary.

a Luca's diet is healthy now, but wasn't when he was younger.
b Luca and his brother have unhealthy diets now.
c Luca's diet has always been quite unhealthy.

2 ▶ 8.6 Listen again. Are the sentences true (T) or false (F)?

1 Luca's mother still tells him to eat more fish. _____
2 When he was younger, Luca ate a lot of vegetables. _____
3 Luca didn't use to like green vegetables. _____
4 Luca's mother made him eat everything on his plate. _____
5 Luca's brother doesn't like vegetables. _____
6 Luca eats uncooked vegetables. _____
7 Luca avoids food with a lot of salt in. _____
8 Luca eats unhealthy food while watching films. _____
9 Luca really dislikes fish. _____
10 Luca's favourite sauces contain a lot of cream. _____

READING

1 Read the blog about cooking. What does it suggest?

a Everyone can learn to cook well with the right instructions.
b There are lots of things that can go wrong when cooking.
c You need lots of equipment in order to cook successfully.

2 Choose the correct options, according to the information in the blog.

1 What is the advantage of cooking a vegetable soup?
  a It is healthy.
  b It is easy.
  c It is vegetarian.

2 Before you start cooking, what should you read?
  a the first line of the recipe
  b the first half of the recipe
  c the whole recipe

3 Which of these things should you check before starting to cook?
  a that you have the right equipment
  b what time it is
  c how many vegetables you need

4 What will a recipe not tell you?
  a which vegetables to use
  b what sort of knife you need
  c exactly how to prepare an onion

5 What does the word *concentrate* in line 20 mean?
  a to do something quickly
  b to focus on one activity
  c to be very careful

6 Why should you add stock to the soup?
  a to make it smell nice
  b to make it less hot
  c to improve the taste

7 What does the last line of the blog suggest?
  a You probably won't eat the soup.
  b You will really enjoy the soup.
  c You will definitely make the soup again.

REVIEW and PRACTICE 8

HOME   BLOG   PODCASTS   ABOUT   CONTACT

Guest blogger Jack tells us how to stay calm in the kitchen.

Keep calm and cook on

If you're new to cooking and want some basic tips, here's a great recipe for a simple but delicious soup. I'll take you step by step through what to do – and what not to do!

1   The first piece of advice is, <u>always</u> read the instructions to the end before you start cooking. You don't want to find out halfway through that you don't have all
5   the ingredients (what if you've run out of noodles?), or some of the equipment (what if your neighbour doesn't own an ice-cream maker either?), or enough time to cook it (oh no, my girlfriend/boyfriend
10 will be here in five minutes and all I've got is a lot of raw vegetables!)

So, after you've read all the instructions, re-read the first line: 'Peel and slice the onion'. Take a sharp kitchen knife, and remove the first brown layer from the onion, and then the second (brownish) layer and then a third. Now, of course the recipe won't tell you when to stop and you
15 don't want to end up with a really tiny onion. Make sure you have plenty of other vegetables – a red pepper, a couple of carrots and a potato (even if slightly green). Chop them into small pieces (and don't worry about the green potato, no one will know once it's cooked).

Next, heat some oil in a pan. But how much oil? And what sort of pan? Pour in enough to just cover the bottom of a medium-sized saucepan. Then add the vegetables. At this point, whatever you do,
20 concentrate! Do not attempt to do anything else! Do not answer your phone! Ignore the doorbell (unless it's the firefighters)! It's so easy to forget to keep an eye on things. Turn the heat down and let the vegetables cook gently for a few minutes. (Don't they smell good?) Then add a litre of water, plus two big spoons of stock (you know, that mysterious salty brown powder at the back of the cupboard – it may not look much, but without it, your soup won't taste … anything like soup). Put
25 a lid on the pan, and leave it for half an hour.

Of course, at this point, you'll forget the instruction not to answer your phone, and will end up talking to a friend for an hour. The final step (nearly) is to taste the 'soup'. And when you discover that even your dog won't eat it … order a takeaway.
29 And that's why you should always read the instructions first!

UNIT 9 Money and shopping

9A LANGUAGE

GRAMMAR: used to

1 Complete the sentences with the words and phrases in the box. You will need to use two of them twice.

> usually   use to   went   did   used to   go

1 Paolo looks different now. He didn't _____ have long hair.
2 On my sixth birthday, I _____ horse riding for the first time.
3 _____ you use to visit your cousins when you were younger?
4 I didn't use to _____ swimming as a child.
5 Yusuf _____ catches the bus to college.
6 She ate lots of ice cream as a child. She _____ love it!
7 Did Daniel _____ be so thin?
8 Lara doesn't _____ go skiing in the summer.

2 Complete the sentences with the correct form of used to and the verb in brackets.

1 I never ate olives as a child. I _____ them. (hate)
2 Did Matheus _____ so hard-working when he was younger? (be)
3 She _____ tennis in her teens, but doesn't now. (play)
4 My grandfather _____ a mobile phone. (not have)
5 Did your parents _____ you bedtime stories? (read)
6 I _____ bright colours in the past. (not wear)
7 Did you _____ the train to London? (take)
8 Aline _____ so much before she went to college. (not go out)

VOCABULARY: Money verbs

3 Order the letters to make money verbs.

1 We aren't rich. We can't **fardof** _____ to stay in that hotel.
2 This café's so expensive. They **ceragh** _____ €8 for a cup of coffee!
3 She has a good job and **searn** _____ more than her husband.
4 Don't forget to **apy kabc** _____ the money Daniel gave you.
5 Jack's going shopping because he **tog apid** _____ yesterday.
6 Don't **awest** _____ your salary on things that you don't need!

4 Complete the sentences with money verbs in the correct form.

1 Can I _____ some money to buy a concert ticket, please?
2 How much did you _____ on that new jacket?
3 I _____ my best friend €10 yesterday to buy lunch.
4 Their house is huge. It must be _____ a fortune.
5 Which _____ more – the blue shirt or the green one?
6 I'm trying to _____ a little money each month to buy a new car.

PRONUNCIATION: used to/use to

5 ▶9.1 Practise saying the sentences. Pay attention to used to and use to. Listen, check and repeat.

1 She didn't use to play tennis.
2 They used to love going to festivals.
3 Did you use to walk to school together?
4 We used to work out at the same gym.
5 He didn't use to like classical music.
6 I remember that you used to enjoy dancing.

50

SKILLS 9B

LISTENING: Identifying attitude and opinion

1 ▶9.2 Listen to Tom and Natalie talking about shopping. Are these sentences true (T) or false (F)?

1 Tom likes shopping online. _____
2 Natalie prefers online shopping. _____
3 Tom thinks online shopping is easy. _____
4 Natalie doesn't like department stores. _____

2 Are the underlined phrases from the conversation opinion (A), feeling (B) or attitude (C)?

1 Yeah, I do most of my shopping online – I much prefer it. _____
2 Sure, you see it's so convenient to shop online. _____
3 I mean, to be honest, shopping for clothes online is the opposite of convenient. _____
4 I wouldn't say that's a big problem. _____
5 I get really fed up waiting! _____
6 I guess I just like shops, especially department stores. _____
7 I enjoy wandering from the clothes section to the kitchen. _____
8 I just remember the crowds and the queues – it was really boring! _____

3 ▶9.2 Listen again and number the fillers 1–8 in order.

a like _____
b I mean _____
c kind of _____
d Er _____
e Well _____
f you see _____
g sort of _____
h So _____

4 ▶9.2 Listen again and complete these sentences and phrases with fillers from exercise 3.

1 Sure, _____, it's so convenient.
2 _____, you just return it, don't you?
3 It's _____ convenient because you don't have to leave your home.
4 You can _____ get everything you want under one roof.
5 And, _____, you can pick things up and see them and feel them.

5 Complete the sentences with shopping words.

1 That jacket was only thirty dollars? Wow! That's an absolute b_ _ _ _ _ _!
2 I bought this bag in the s_ _ _ _ for half the usual price!
3 Students get a d_ _ _ _ _ _ _ _ of 20% in all our shops.
4 The trousers didn't fit so I sent them back and got a r_ _ _ _ _.
5 I asked the shop assistant if I could e_ _ _ _ _ _ _ _ the jacket for a larger size.
6 Are you paying with cash or by c_ _ _ _ _ card?
7 I need to try this suit on. Where's the nearest c_ _ _ _ _ _ _ room?
8 Sometimes I used to go w_ _ _ _ _ shopping with no money in my pocket. I just looked at all the lovely things.
9 There was such a long q_ _ _ _ to pay that I decided not to wait.
10 I paid for the items and the cashier gave me a r_ _ _ _ _ _.

51

9C LANGUAGE

GRAMMAR: The passive

1 Choose the correct options to complete the sentences.

1 The wallet was ____ yesterday by a member of the public.
   a hand in   b handed in   c to hand in
2 This park ____ by many people.
   a isn't used   b isn't using   c doesn't use
3 When was the problem ____?
   a discovering   b discovered   c discover
4 In summer, dinner ____ in the garden.
   a served   b is served   c serving
5 A number of mistakes ____ during the investigation.
   a was made   b made   c were made
6 Over 300 people ____ to the party.
   a were invited   b invited   c was invited

2 Complete the text about the history of money. Use the present or past passive form of the verbs in brackets.

It ¹_____ (say) by many people today that 'money makes the world go round'. It's certainly hard to imagine life without it, but money ²_____ (not invent) until several thousand years ago in China. Tiny models of weapons and tools ³_____ (use) there as money. Before that, full-size tools and weapons ⁴_____ (exchange) for goods and services in a system called 'barter'. The first coins ⁵_____ (produce) 2,500 years ago in Lydia, in what is now Turkey. They ⁶_____ (make) from 'electrum', a mixture of gold and silver. The first paper banknotes ⁷_____ (print) by the Chinese at around the same time. Fast forward in time, and today most goods and services ⁸_____ (buy) with credit and debit cards, or even using smartphone 'wallets'. Huge sums ⁹_____ (send) from bank to bank without anyone touching a single banknote. Virtual currencies like Bitcoin ¹⁰_____ (accept) in some shops and online. Will notes and coins disappear completely within our lifetime?

3 Complete the sentences with the passive form of the verbs in the box. Use the tense in brackets.

discover   eat   write   invent
wash   bake   steal   paint

1 The planet Uranus _____ by Sir William Herschel in 1781. (past simple)
2 Bread _____ every morning in our own bakery. (present simple)
3 I don't have a bike now. It _____ last week from outside the school. (past simple)
4 The picture _____ by Pablo Picasso in 1933. (past simple)
5 His car always looks perfect because it _____ every week. (present simple)
6 This song _____ by John Grant. (past simple)
7 Lunch _____ in the main dining room. (present simple)
8 The first electric train _____ by a German in 1879. (past simple)

PRONUNCIATION: Sentence stress

4 ▶ 9.3 Underline the three words that you think will be stressed in each sentence. Listen, check and repeat.

1 This soup is made with peppers.
2 The children are taught by their parents.
3 These plants are grown by my father.
4 The message was posted on Facebook.
5 Those houses were built in 1975.
6 That race was won by her cousin.

SKILLS 9D

WRITING: Writing a formal email

1 Read Elisabeth's email complaining about a flat-screen TV she has bought. Choose the correct words and phrases.

To: info@tvs2go.com

RE: Recent order (H23 100-A)

¹*Dear Sir/Madam / Hello*,

I am writing ²*to tell you about / with regard to* the flat-screen TV that ³*a man installed / was installed* in my house last Thursday.

Firstly, ⁴*someone delivered the TV / the TV was delivered* at 3 p.m., not at 10 a.m. as agreed. Secondly, as the man left, I noticed that some wires were hanging down at the back of the TV. When I ⁵*pointed this out / told him about it*, he was extremely rude. Although he agreed to fix the wires, he ⁶*did not / didn't* check that the TV was working correctly.

⁷*I'm / I am* sure you will agree that this level of service is ⁸*terrible / unacceptable*, and that a full refund of the delivery charge would be appropriate. Could you please arrange ⁹*to pay the money / for the money to be paid* within a week?

I look forward to hearing from you soon.

¹⁰*Regards / Bye for now*

Elisabeth Miller

---

2 Match the correct options 1–10 from exercise 1 with these features of formal emails.

a full forms, not contractions   ___ ___
b formal words and expressions   ___ ___ ___
c passives to avoid being personal   ___ ___ ___
d a formal greeting   ___
e a formal ending   ___

3 Complete the sentences with nouns made from these verbs.

| order   argue   increase   deliver |
| improve   discover   discuss |
| decide   organize   inform |

1 Last week I made the _____ to purchase several items from your website.
2 The _____ on your website was not correct.
3 I was not aware of the price _____ when I ordered the product.
4 I was shocked by the _____ that several parts were broken.
5 After a _____ with one of your staff, I am still not satisfied.
6 I did not expect to become involved in an _____ with one of your sales team.
7 Poor service will damage the reputation of your _____.
8 Your company needs to make a great _____ in the quality of its goods.
9 I will expect _____ of a replacement within a week.
10 Please send me a full refund for my _____.

4 Write a formal email complaining about a product you have bought recently.

- Include paragraphs giving the reason for writing, explaining the situation and saying what action you want taken.
- Remember to use the features in exercise 2.
- Use the sentences in exercise 3 for ideas.

9 REVIEW and PRACTICE

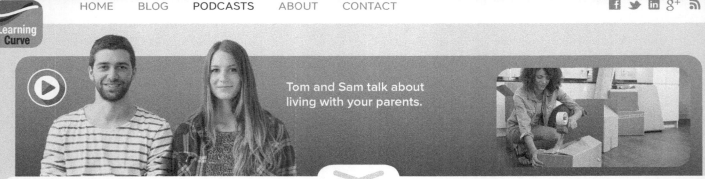

HOME   BLOG   PODCASTS   ABOUT   CONTACT

Tom and Sam talk about living with your parents.

LISTENING

1 ▶ 9.4 Listen to the podcast. Tick (✓) the correct statement.

a Sonia moved out of her parents' house because there were too many rules. ____
b Sonia's parents gave her money to help with her college fees. ____
c Sonia went to live with her parents because she wasn't earning enough money. ____
d Sonia couldn't afford to go to college so she got a job instead. ____

2 ▶ 9.4 Listen again. Complete the sentences with one or two words.

1 One of the _____ of Sonia's life was getting her degree.
2 Sonia was scared that she might trip and _____.
3 Sonia didn't know how she was going to _____ her college fees.
4 Sonia owed a total of _____ euros.
5 It took Sonia _____ to get a good job.
6 Sonia gave her parents money for _____ and _____.
7 When she was _____, Sonia didn't like her parents' rules.

READING

1 Read the blog about money and relationships. Choose the best summary.

a People often split up because they can't agree about money. You should talk about money with your partner, and if you have very different attitudes, it's best not to get married.
b It's hard to change people's attitudes to money, but if you understand how your partner feels, you won't feel so angry if they waste money you wanted to save.
c Attitudes to money are very important. You should try to understand how your partner feels and if you have different attitudes, you should try to find ways to stop them causing arguments.

2 Tick (✓) the correct sentences, according to the information in the blog.

1 Things that happen in our lives can affect how we feel about money. ____
2 Attitudes to money are more important than someone's personality. ____
3 People from poor families may not feel happy about borrowing money. ____
4 Attitudes to money can change if a relationship lasts a long time. ____
5 Couples should be honest with each other when they talk about money. ____
6 We should discuss the emotional reasons why money is important to us. ____
7 People with very different attitudes to money can't have a successful relationship. ____
8 Each person in a couple should pay the same amount of the bills. ____
9 Philip and Christa wanted to buy a home together. ____
10 When Philip saw Christa spending a lot of money, he thought their relationship wouldn't work. ____

HOME   BLOG   PODCASTS   ABOUT   CONTACT

Tom writes about money and relationships.

Money – how to stop it ruining your relationship

Experts say that the main reason long-term couples split up is money – and the arguments it causes. Our attitudes to money often come from our life experiences – and that makes them difficult to change. Someone brought up in a poor family may get really anxious about owing money, and be horrified at the idea of 'wasting' it on things they don't think are necessary. So what can we do to stop money ruining a relationship?

'We all have a money personality,' says life coach Jo Handslip. 'If we're thinking of a long-term relationship with someone, we need to get to know that side of them just as well as the other parts of their character. And whatever we may hope, we also need to understand that their money personality isn't likely to change.'

The most important thing a couple can do is talk about money openly. 'This isn't about money simply as a means of buying things,' says Jo. 'It's about what money represents to us.' She says that couples should start by trying to identify what each of them associates with money, like success, security, independence, power, fun or being free from stress.

Once they understand this, they can try to make their different attitudes work together. So, if one of you loves the freedom and excitement of spending money and the other one wants the security of having savings, maybe you should agree to share the cost of bills, but keep the rest of your money separate. That way, the 'spender' can only spend their own money, and the 'saver' can feel secure. Or you could agree a maximum amount you can spend without asking your partner.

Philip Walker knows all about the problems money can cause. He and his girlfriend Christa split up just two weeks before their wedding! 'We were saving up for a flat, so we agreed that the ceremony should be fairly small. But then I found out that instead of spending our savings on the wedding, Christa was going out celebrating with her friends in expensive clubs, and buying loads of new clothes when she already had more than she needed. She'd buy the same dress or pairs of shoes in three different colours because she couldn't decide which she liked best! We ended up having a huge argument. In the end, seeing her throw our money away made me feel that she didn't see a future for us together.'

UNIT 10 Sport and fitness

10A LANGUAGE

GRAMMAR: Past perfect

1 Choose the correct tenses to complete the sentences.

1 That evening, I was tired because I ____ ten kilometres in the afternoon.
   a had run   b ran   c was running
2 We ____ hungry because we'd already eaten.
   a weren't being   b hadn't been   c weren't
3 By the time we arrived at the theatre, the play ____.
   a had already started   b already started
   c was already starting
4 When I met Lara I was sure I ____ her somewhere before.
   a saw   b was seeing   c had seen
5 I'd put on a thick jacket and I ____ too hot later.
   a was being   b had been   c was
6 I ____ how the movie would end because I had read the book.
   a had known   b knew   c know
7 He had cut his finger as he ____ the meat.
   a was preparing   b preparing   c had prepared
8 We arrived late at the party, so most of the food ____.
   a had gone   b went   c was going
9 I didn't have any money with me as I ____ my wallet.
   a didn't bring   b hadn't brought
   c wasn't bringing
10 Camilla said she had met Igor while she ____ around Europe.
   a travelled   b was travelling   c had travelled

2 Complete the sentences with the verb pairs. Write one past simple and one past perfect form in each sentence.

> say / go   live / move   know / go   meet / know
> pass / study   be / lose   finish / leave   be / leave

1 After we _____ our dinner, we _____ the restaurant.
2 The teacher _____ cross because I _____ my work at home.
3 He _____ stressed because he _____ his phone.
4 Jorge _____ all his exams because he _____ hard all year.
5 I _____ Javier once at Laura's house, so I _____ who he was.
6 She _____ in Italy for three years before she _____ to France.
7 Eduardo _____ most of the people at the club because he _____ there before.
8 After I _____ goodnight, I _____ to bed.

VOCABULARY: Sports and competitions

3 Order the letters to make words that match the definitions.

1 to behave dishonestly in order to achieve something THEAC _____
2 someone who watches people playing sport TRAPECOTS _____
3 to win a point CROSE _____
4 someone who does sports like running and jumping THELATE _____
5 the person who controls the game FREEREE _____
6 a prize for winning a competition HOTPRY _____

4 Complete the words.

1 She hopes to get a gold m___ ___ ___ at the next Olympics.
2 Our team needs another goal to d___ ___ ___ the match.
3 There was a huge c___ ___ ___ watching last night's game.
4 Don't forget to w___ ___ ___ u___ before you go running.
5 Would you like to t___ ___ ___ p___ ___ ___ in our swimming competition?
6 You can't g___ ___ ___ u___ now. You're nearly at the finishing line!

PRONUNCIATION: 'd/hadn't

5 ▶10.1 Practise saying the sentences. Pay attention to the pronunciation of 'd and hadn't. Listen, check and repeat.

1 She'd already won the match.
2 He hadn't taken part in the competition.
3 We'd lost both games.
4 They certainly hadn't cheated.
5 We hadn't scored yet.
6 They'd drawn in the semi-final.

READING: Finding information in a text

WEARABLE FITNESS DEVICES

News
Reviews
Fitness trackers
Watches
Forum

Fitness trackers

A | Wearable fitness is everywhere you look. There are now hundreds of types of fitness tracker on the market, the simplest of which simply count how many steps you take in a day. The more sophisticated models record your heartbeat, your food intake, your skin temperature, even how often you snore in your sleep! They allow you to observe and measure details about your own body that previously only doctors were able to see. Which, of course, is fascinating. But apart from providing interest in our lives, are these (often expensive) gadgets worth it? Do they serve any real purpose, other than making a nice profit for a number of companies?

B | Well, it turns out that in a lot of cases they probably do. Not because fitness trackers provide 100% accurate data. (If you try out two different brands of fitness tracker, it's very likely that you'll get two quite different step counts over the course of the day.) But because they're always there – often on your wrist – reminding you that you haven't moved or slept enough recently. Turn on your phone and a figure will pop up, telling you how well you're doing. (Some models will even tell you how well your friends are doing!) And that's what most of us need – a constant reminder that we need to do better.

C | And let's not forget that they're fun. Without a fitness tracker, we may know that we should use our legs more and our wheels less, but we may not actually do anything about it. When we wear a device that rewards us with a 'ping' every time we reach our target step count, we are more likely to get off the bus two stops away from work and walk. Daily routines become a sort of game we play with ourselves, and who wouldn't that appeal to?

1 Read the text about gadgets that measure your fitness, then match paragraphs A–C with three of summaries 1–6.

1 A disadvantage of wearable fitness devices. ____
2 What do fitness trackers do? ____
3 The companies that make these fitness devices. ____
4 The enjoyment factor of wearable fitness devices. ____
5 The author's experience of these fitness devices. ____
6 Why wearable fitness devices are useful. ____

2 Read the questions and match them to paragraphs A–C. Then write short answers. There are two questions for each paragraph.

1 What part of the body do you wear some of these devices on? _____
2 What do we all know we should do less of? _____
3 How many different kinds of device are available? _____
4 Where can you look at the information these devices collect? _____
5 What activity do we know we should do more often? _____
6 What can some devices count while you are in bed? _____

3 Complete the sentences with *example*, *for*, *like* or *such*.

1 We can all get more exercise, _____ instance, by walking rather than driving.
2 With this device daily routines, _____ going upstairs and walking home from the station, can be fun.
3 Everyone can now monitor aspects of their body's behaviour, _____ as their heartbeat and temperature.
4 We can find out, for _____, how deeply we're sleeping

10C LANGUAGE

GRAMMAR: Reported speech

1 Complete the sentences with *said* or *told*.

1 She _____ she would call me at the weekend.
2 Nerea and Lucia _____ me they had seen you at the gym.
3 She _____ me that Gabriel had gone to the meeting.
4 He _____ that Yasmin would take Lola to the airport.
5 Isaac _____ he would talk to Miguel about the problem.
6 He _____ that Sophia liked her colleagues.
7 Paula _____ me she had met you at the wedding.
8 He _____ me that Livia wasn't coming.

2 Use the prompts to rewrite the sentences in reported speech.

1 'I'll phone you from the station.'
My sister / tell me / she phone me / from the station
_____.

2 'Dad can cook dinner for you and Laura.'
My mum / say / Dad cook / dinner for us
_____.

3 'I didn't see Luke in town on Saturday.'
He / tell me / he / not see / Luke in town on Saturday
_____.

4 'I've just bought a new computer.'
Maria / say / she buy / a new computer
_____.

5 'We're going to move to France.'
He / tell me / they going to move / to France
_____.

6 'I haven't made up my mind.'
She / say / she / not make up / her mind
_____.

7 'I'm meeting Davi on Friday.'
Vitor / tell me / he meet Davi / on Friday
_____.

8 'Alba loves going for walks.'
He / say / Alba love / going for walks
_____.

VOCABULARY: Parts of the body

3 Match parts of the body a–j with the definitions 1–8.

1 This is in your head and controls how you think. _____
2 This helps your arm to bend. _____
3 These are the soft edges of the mouth. _____
4 This helps your leg to bend. _____
5 This part of the body contains the heart. _____
6 This is the soft part of the front of the body, above your legs. _____
7 These are the two parts of your body at the tops of your arms. _____
8 This is just above your foot at the bottom of your leg. _____

a shoulders   e stomach   i elbow
b thumb   f lips   j knee
c chest   g forehead
d brain   h ankle

4 Complete the words.

1 After running, the m___ ___ ___ ___ ___ ___ in my legs were tired.
2 She'd broken a b___ ___ ___ in her foot and couldn't walk.
3 Azra was wearing a pretty scarf around her n___ ___ ___.
4 A healthy diet and regular exercise is good for your h___ ___ ___ ___ .
5 He was wearing sandals, so I could see his t___ ___ ___.
6 After a few days in the sun, her s___ ___ ___ was really brown.
7 Why is she pointing a f___ ___ ___ ___ ___ at me?
8 Vito has an expensive-looking watch on his left w___ ___ ___ ___.

PRONUNCIATION: Weak form of *that*

5 ▶10.2 Listen to the sentences. Is *that* strong (S) or weak (W)? Listen, check and repeat.

1 Zeynep said that she was leaving. _____
2 Is that your cousin over there? _____
3 That's not what I said! _____
4 Ismail told me that I was wrong. _____
5 Pam said that the party started at eight. _____
6 Could you give me that book, please? _____
7 Beatriz told Clara that she was angry. _____
8 Sara likes the blue bike, but I like that one. _____

SPEAKING: Making enquiries

1 ▶10.3 Gabriella is a guest at an expensive hotel. Listen to her conversation with the receptionist. Are the statements true (T) or false (F)?

1 Gabriella didn't know that the hotel has a fitness suite. ____
2 The exercise room has a lot of equipment that guests can use. ____
3 Gabriella wants someone to show her the exercise suite. ____
4 Guests don't have to pay to use the swimming pool. ____
5 The swimming pool is closed at night. ____
6 The receptionist will send an extra towel to Gabriella's room. ____

2 ▶10.3 Listen again. You will hear seven of these phrases. Write G (Gabriella) or R (receptionist).

a Is there anything else I can help you with? ____
b Could you give me some information about ..., please? ____
c Just one more thing. ____
d Excuse me, could you tell me ...? ____
e I'd also like to ask about ... ____
f Does that sound OK? ____
g I was told ... Is that true? ... ____
h I'll ... if you want. ____
i Shall I ...? ____
j Can I just double-check? Do you ...? ____
k Would you like me to ...? ____
l Could I speak to someone about ...? ____
m I was hoping you could help me. ____

3 Put the phrases from exercise 2 into the correct categories.

1 starting an enquiry politely ____
2 asking for additional information ____
3 being helpful ____

4 ▶10.4 Use the phrases in exercise 2 to complete these conversations. There may be more than one possible answer. Then listen and say the missing part aloud.

1 In a sports shop

A Good morning. Can I help you?
B Hello. ¹_____ trainers, please? I'm looking for a pair for long-distance running.
A Yes, we have several suitable pairs. Shall I bring some for you to try?
B That would be great, thanks.
  ²_____ waterproof jackets.
A We don't have any available at the moment, but here's a catalogue. You can order them online. Does that sound OK?

2 At the gym

A Excuse me, can I get Pilates lessons here?
B Yes, we have several teachers.
  ³_____ give you a list?
A Great, thanks.
B You can call them to arrange a time.
  ⁴_____?
A Yes, perfect, thanks.
B Here's the list. ⁵_____?
A No, that's everything. Thanks for your help.

10 REVIEW and PRACTICE

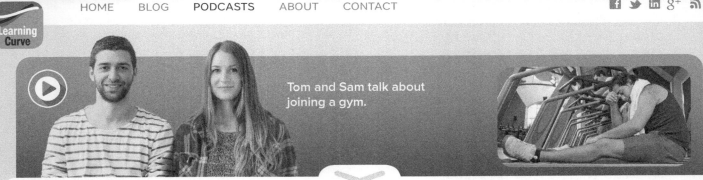

LISTENING

1 ▶10.5 Listen to the podcast. Tick (✓) the parts of the body which are mentioned.

a foot _____
b neck _____
c muscle _____
d ankle _____
e wrist _____
f stomach _____
g shoulder _____
h bone _____
i heart _____
j knee _____

2 ▶10.5 Listen again. Choose the correct options to complete the sentences.

1 How long has Hakim been going to the sports centre?
  a about one year
  b about two years
  c about five years
2 For his height, Hakim
  a weighs too little.
  b weighs the right amount.
  c weighs too much.
3 Hakim wants a workout that's good for his
  a stomach.
  b muscles.
  c heart.
4 Hakim says that he
  a has always been active.
  b has never done much exercise.
  c has never injured himself.
5 Hakim had to have an operation when he was
  a eight.
  b eleven.
  c twenty.
6 What happened while Hakim was skiing?
  a He got an injury to his leg.
  b He damaged part of his arm.
  c He caused a serious accident.

READING

1 Read the blog about sports injuries. Choose the best summary.

a Peter didn't prepare properly for his run and, because of his injury, he will never be able to run again.
b Peter hadn't realized there was a problem with his ankle and made things worse by doing more exercise.
c Peter wasn't used to doing much exercise, and badly hurt his ankle soon after starting his run.

2 Choose the correct options to complete the sentences.

1 According to Peter, after a sports injury you feel
  a upset and annoyed.
  b surprised and frightened.
  c tired and embarrassed.
2 Peter hurt his ankle
  a when he got up one day.
  b while he was running.
  c when he was preparing to run.
3 Peter's doctor told him
  a to stop running for a few weeks.
  b to run shorter distances.
  c to stop running completely.
4 Peter had
  a had a few injuries in the past.
  b never injured himself before.
  c only recently started running.
5 Peter says that stress
  a means it takes longer to recover from injury.
  b is hard for most people to control.
  c can make it difficult for him to run.
6 Peter says that he
  a thought his ankle would never get better.
  b was impatient to recover as quickly as possible.
  c did what his doctor had told him to do.

REVIEW and PRACTICE 10

HOME BLOG PODCASTS ABOUT CONTACT

Guest blogger Kate gets some advice on recovering from sports injuries.

How I got back on track

We all know we should do plenty of exercise and many of us have a favourite sport or activity. But what happens if you suffer an injury and can't do the sport you love? How do you cope with it and how do you recover from it? Peter Jackson, sports coach and runner, told us about his experience of being injured.

It's tough. You feel so many negative emotions. You're angry because you can't do your sport. You feel disappointed because your body has failed you. And you're bored because you can't do what you want to do!

One morning last year I got up and noticed a problem with my right ankle. It was a slight pain at first and I thought it would go away. I'd done a long run the day before – a few miles more than usual – and thought perhaps that was why. Anyway, I went running, as usual. I'd done everything properly to prepare. I'd put a bandage on for support and, of course, I'd warmed up before starting.

But as I ran, the pain got worse and worse and after three miles I had to give up and go home. The next day, I saw my doctor who told me that I'd injured my ankle quite badly and that I would have to rest it for four to six weeks – that meant no running at all! It was a bit of a shock. Until that point, I'd run every day for the previous four or five years, with no problems. Suddenly, I had to learn new habits. Most importantly, I had to start listening to my body – it was telling me to rest.

Of course, at first I felt very stressed by not being able to run, but I learned to manage that. It's often said that stress is caused by the feeling that we can't control a situation, and stress stops the body from getting better. So the first thing I had to understand was that I was in control because I was helping myself to get better. I couldn't take part in running any more, but by resting my ankle and doing the exercises that the doctor had shown me, I was taking part in my recovery. I learned to be patient – to accept that it takes time to get better – and above all, I learned to be positive – to believe that I would recover.

UNIT
11 At home

11A | **LANGUAGE**

GRAMMAR: -ing/infinitive verb patterns

1 Choose the correct options to complete the sentences.

1 I have arranged _____ Rino this evening.
   a meeting   b to meet

2 Have you finished _____ your bedroom yet?
   a decorating   b to decorate

3 Frankie can't stand _____ early.
   a getting up   b to get up

4 The firm is planning _____ its factory in Ireland.
   a closing   b to close

5 Oh no! I forgot _____ my passport!
   a bringing   b to bring

6 Would you mind _____ dinner tonight?
   a cooking   b to cook

7 Gary hopes _____ a place in the team.
   a getting   b to get

8 Do you fancy _____ to the beach today?
   a going   b to go

9 I can't imagine _____ a marathon!
   a running   b to run

10 Unfortunately, I can't afford _____ a holiday this year.
   a having   b to have

2 Complete the text with the correct form of the verbs in the box.

> get   move   tell   play
> visit   stay   hang out   pay

Last year, I decided ¹_____ to another city. I was bored with my job, and I wanted a change. I'm the sort of person that hates ²_____ in the same place for too long. Luckily, I managed ³_____ a new job quite quickly. My new firm even offered ⁴_____ my rent for three months while I looked for a place to buy. The only problem was my great friend, Sol. He kept ⁵_____ me that I would be lonely and that I'd miss ⁶_____ with him and our other friends. I did feel sorry about leaving Sol, but I knew I'd make new friends quite quickly. I love ⁷_____ football and joining a team is always a good way to meet people. However, I promised ⁸_____ Sol as often as I could, and I've kept my promise.

VOCABULARY: Household objects

3 Order the letters to make words that match the descriptions.

1 It keeps you warm in bed. EVTUD   _____

2 It is in the bathroom and holds water.
  SHAW INSAB   _____

3 You put dirty clothes in it. GASWNHI CHANMIE _____

4 You keep your clothes in it. THESC FO REWARS
                                             _____

5 They are made of thin material and go on a bed. THESES _____

6 It keeps your house warm. ANCTLER THIGANE
                                             _____

4 Complete the crossword.

Across

3 All the dirty plates need to go in the _____.

7 I sleep best with a soft _____ under my head.

8 The cake must be cooked, so take it out of the _____.

9 It was cold, so we put an extra _____ on the bed.

Down

1 If you're not comfortable on the sofa, put a _____ behind your back.

2 Pia had a _____ full of beautiful clothes.

4 A _____ is a small carpet.

5 I turned on both _____ to fill the bath quickly.

6 Is the _____ hot enough yet to do my shirt?

PRONUNCIATION: Sentence stress

5 ▶ 11.1 Listen to these sentences and repeat them. Pay attention to the way *to* is pronounced.

1 Guy can't afford to buy a new laptop.

2 The children enjoy playing in the park.

3 We plan to meet our friends at eight.

4 I don't fancy going to the cinema.

5 I forgot to lock the door.

6 Sylvie doesn't want to come with us.

62

SKILLS 11B

LISTENING: Understanding and interpreting information

1 ▶11.2 Read the sentences and look at the underlined words. Think about other words that the speakers might use. Then listen to the conversation. Are the sentences True (T) or False (F)?

1 Johnny is <u>extremely tired</u> after doing the housework. ____
2 Johnny has <u>cleaned</u> the kitchen floor. ____
3 Marta says Johnny's housemates will be <u>very pleased</u> with him. ____
4 As part of Marta and Sara's <u>agreement</u>, Marta cleans the house. ____
5 Marta tells Johnny she <u>hates</u> cleaning. ____
6 Marta's housemate, Sara, <u>is extremely keen on</u> food. ____
7 Marta says the meals that she cooks are <u>really good</u>. ____
8 Marta says she spends <u>a lot of time</u> deciding what to cook. ____

2 ▶11.2 Listen again and check and write the actual words the speakers use.

1 extremely tired _____
2 cleaned _____
3 very pleased _____
4 agreement _____
5 hates _____
6 is extremely keen on _____
7 really good _____
8 a lot of time _____

3 Read the short conversations. Write the words that the speakers don't say.

1 A She was angry.
  B No, she wasn't. _____
2 A Do you think Maria's happy at work?
  B Not so sure about that! _____
3 A What's wrong?
  B Computer's not working! _____
4 A You look really stressed.
  B Yes! Big problem with the arrangements for Saturday! _____
5 A Sara doesn't like cooking, I'm guessing?
  B No, hates it! _____

4 Match a–e with missing words 1–5 in exercise 3.

a pronouns ____
b articles ____
c *be* and auxiliary verbs ____
d *There is/are* ____
e avoid repeating words ____

5 Match the two parts of the sentences.

1 We'll need to lay ____
2 Tom said he was mopping ____
3 Could you hang out ____
4 I completely forgot to water ____
5 After we finished eating, we loaded ____
6 Ella got up and had breakfast, then made ____
7 He dropped some food and had to vacuum ____
8 Don't forget to take out ____

a the plants in the garden.
b these clothes to dry, please?
c the rubbish, will you?
d the carpet.
e the dishwasher.
f the bathroom floor when I called.
g her bed.
h the dinner table for six people.

63

11C — LANGUAGE

GRAMMAR: Articles

1 Match the two parts of the sentences.

1 I would really love a _____
2 Paul said he would like an _____
3 I think I will enjoy the _____
4 We could have _____
5 Esther talked a lot about _____
6 Laura explained the _____
7 Rick told me about an _____
8 Maria described a _____

a book you told us about.
b route to Bill's house.
c drink.
d village in China.
e old friend who was a musician.
f orange.
g politics.
h breakfast before we go.

2 Complete the sentences with the correct article or –
(no article).

1 Viv goes to the doctor's twice _____ year.
2 We went to _____ amazing concert last night.
3 I'm a bit scared of _____ dogs.
4 She gave _____ taxi driver a big tip.
5 Patsy has to go to _____ hospital tomorrow.
6 I usually have sandwiches for _____ lunch.
7 _____ Monday is the first day of the working week.
8 They need to go into town before _____ bank shuts.
9 What's _____ name of Pete's girlfriend?
10 My sister is _____ engineer.

3 Read the review and choose the correct sequence of articles, A, B or C.

'Spectacles' review *****

This week we're reviewing Spectacles, ¹_____ pair of sunglasses that can take ²_____ videos. ³_____ product is made by ⁴_____ video and messaging app, Snapchat. ⁵_____ videos are ⁶_____ unusual shape: they're round, similar to human vision. Spectacles' 10-second video clips are sent via Bluetooth to users' smartphones.

A	1 –	2 –	3 –	4 the	5 –	6 a
B	1 a	2 –	3 The	4 the	5 The	6 an
C	1 a	2 the	3 The	4 –	5 The	6 the

VOCABULARY: Words to describe materials and clothes

4 Complete the sentences with the words in the box.

silk   fur   casual   wooden   wool   metal

1 I'm an animal lover, so I don't wear _____ coats.
2 You need to polish _____ jewellery to make it shine.
3 It's best to wash _____ shirts by hand.
4 We gave Helga an unusual _____ ring for her birthday.
5 In winter, I wear a _____ jumper to keep warm.
6 Joe packed some _____ clothes for his holiday.

5 Complete the words.

1 My sister is a vegetarian and won't even buy l___ ___ ___ ___ ___ ___ shoes.
2 You should wear s___ ___ ___ ___ clothes for an interview.
3 In summer Felipe prefers short-sleeved c___ ___ ___ ___ ___ shirts.
4 We aren't allowed to wear d___ ___ ___ ___ jeans to work.
5 Are these trousers too t___ ___ ___ ___? I think I need a larger size.
6 She didn't buy the skirt with flowers on because she wanted something p___ ___ ___ ___.

PRONUNCIATION: *the*

6 ▶11.3 Listen and circle the pronunciation of *the* that you hear. Listen, check and repeat.

1	We need to catch **the** early train..	/ðə/	/ði:/
2	Where are all **the** other people?	/ðə/	/ði:/
3	What time does **the** concert start?	/ðə/	/ði:/
4	Shall we meet at **the** usual place?	/ðə/	/ði:/
5	Don't forget to bring **the** tickets.	/ðə/	/ði:/
6	His house is painted pink on **the** outside.	/ðə/	/ði:/
7	How did you get on in **the** exam?	/ðə/	/ði:/
8	I've spilled juice on **the** carpet.	/ðə/	/ði:/

SKILLS 11D

WRITING: Making writing interesting

1 Read David's description of his friend's house and complete it with the words in the box.

so (x 2)   because   but   although   however   and   also   as well

Michael's house

My friend Michael lives with his parents in a big modern house just outside the city. I think it's an excellent place to live ¹_____ it's really peaceful there, ²_____ it's still easy to get into the city on the bus.

Michael's mum is a keen gardener, and they have a gorgeous garden with lots of flowers. It ³_____ has a large oval swimming pool, where we often hang out at the weekends.

⁴_____ the rooms in Michael's house are spacious, they're still very comfortable. In Michael's room, there's an old leather sofa ⁵_____ lots of soft red velvet cushions. There's a lovely thick rug ⁶_____.

All the rooms have big windows ⁷_____ they're bright and airy. ⁸_____, most of them have thick, black blinds, ⁹_____ you can make the rooms dark if you want to. That's especially useful in the sitting room, where we often watch movies.

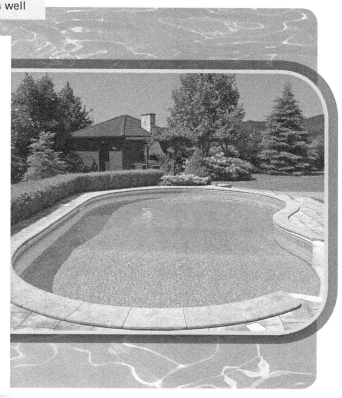

2 Order the adjectives to complete the sentences.

1 He owns a(n) _____ bed.
(huge/amazing/square)
2 Her bedroom has _____ curtains.
(pale green/silk/fashionable)
3 My house contains a _____ living area.
(spacious/modern)
4 Their home is full of _____ furniture.
(old/oak/beautiful)
5 She uses _____ sheets on the beds.
(Egyptian/white/cotton)
6 I don't like the _____ window frames.
(horrible/plastic/modern)
7 On the table there is a _____ vase.
(Chinese/large/round)
8 The dining room has a _____ carpet.
(blue/gorgeous)

3 Find these words in the text and match them with synonyms a–d.

1 spacious   ____
2 gorgeous   ____
3 hang out   ____
4 get into   ____

a spend time
b reach
c large
d beautiful

4 Find two examples in the text of *where* and an example of what you can do there. Then complete 1–4 with your own ideas.

1 Greg's house has a gorgeous long garden, where
_____.
2 Anna's cottage has an old red living room, where
_____.
3 Peter's apartment has an enormous square balcony, where
_____.
4 There is a wonderful modern kitchen, where
_____.

5 Write a description of a home you like.
- Use adjectives in the correct order.
- Use synonyms to avoid repeating words.
- Use linkers to give reasons and results (*so, because, that's why*), to contrast information (*but, although, however*) or add information (*and, also, too, as well*).
- Include a sentence with *where* and what you can do in a particular place.

65

11 REVIEW and PRACTICE

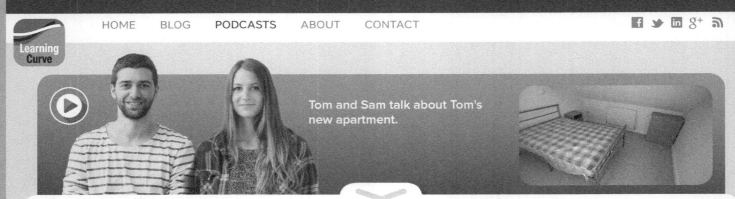

LISTENING

1 ▶ 11.4 Listen to the podcast. Number these things in the order Tom mentions them.

a wardrobe _____
b sofa _____
c freezer _____
d central heating _____
e kitchen _____
f duvet _____
g fridge _____
h chest of drawers _____

2 ▶ 11.4 Listen again. Is each statement correct (YES) or incorrect (NO)?

		Yes	No
1	Tom has been in his new home for less than a month.	☐	☐
2	Tom moved in on the coldest day of the year.	☐	☐
3	Tom had to go to bed early to keep warm.	☐	☐
4	Tom was pleased the central heating was soon fixed.	☐	☐
5	Tom hasn't had time to put his clothes in the wardrobe.	☐	☐
6	At the moment, Tom doesn't mind not having a freezer.	☐	☐
7	Tom would prefer different wallpaper in his new home.	☐	☐
8	Tom is confident that Sam will really like his apartment.	☐	☐

READING

1 Read the blog about house-sharing. Tick (✓) the correct sentences, according to the information in the blog.

1 House prices are rising, so more people share houses today than ever before. _____
2 People often need to share houses, but there can be problems. _____
3 You need to make sure your new housemate can afford to live there. _____
4 Feelings are important, but you can take practical steps to make sharing a house successful. _____
5 If you can't share with someone you know, you should meet them before you move in together. _____
6 You should make a list of important things about where you are going to live. _____

2 Are the sentences true (T), false (F), or is there not enough information to decide (N)?

1 Many people have bad experiences with housemates. _____
2 Mollie's housemate didn't know how to use their washing machine. _____
3 Jamie liked his housemate's snake. _____
4 A lot of people move into houses they can't really afford. _____
5 Becky's housemate was often late with her rent. _____
6 It doesn't matter why someone left the last place they lived. _____
7 Daniel didn't like the sort of music his housemates played. _____
8 If you don't feel comfortable with someone, you should find out where they lived before. _____
9 Websites can be a good place to find house-sharing opportunities. _____
10 At a speed housemating event, you can immediately see basic information about people. _____

REVIEW and PRACTICE 11

HOME BLOG PODCASTS ABOUT CONTACT

Guest blogger Penny explains how to find the perfect housemate.

The highs and lows of house-sharing

You want to leave home, but you can't afford your own apartment. What do you do? Sharing accommodation with other people in the same situation is the obvious answer, but how do you find those people, and how do you know you will get on with them? The internet is full of horror stories – here are a few of them!

'One of my housemates never changed his sheets,' says 21-year-old Mollie Goodman. 'Eventually the whole house started to smell!' 23-year-old Jamie King also had bad experiences. 'In one place I lived, this guy moved in and brought a huge snake with him. Even worse, he filled the freezer with dead mice to feed it!'

Of course, money's another issue. You might be embarrassed to ask someone how they plan to pay the rent, but you don't want to end up like Becky. Her housemate claimed to be an actor, but the truth was that she was usually out of work. Not only did she rarely pay her rent on time, she also thought it was OK to use Becky's shampoo, drink her milk and even 'borrow' her clothes (without asking, of course!).

If you're the person moving into a house, find out why the last person left. Maybe, like Daniel Mills, 24, it was because the others were all in a band together – and rehearsed at home! 'I never got a moment's peace – it was terrible!' he says. If you're the one with a spare room, <u>always</u> ask for references from the people they lived with before. And listen to your heart – if you have a bad feeling about someone, just walk away. But listen to your head as well – even if someone seems great, get an agreement in writing.

Most of us would prefer to live with someone we know, but that's not always possible, especially if you've moved to a new city. Online house-share sites are a good place to start. But one thing everyone agrees on is that you must meet the people you're going to live with face to face before you move in. Because this can take a lot of time, 'speed housemating' events are getting more and more popular – when people with rooms can meet people who want to rent. Everyone wears a sticker showing their budget and where they want to live. It's like speed dating, but with a front door key thrown in!

UNIT 12

People and relationships

12A LANGUAGE

GRAMMAR: Defining relative clauses

1 Choose the correct options to complete the sentences.

1 Did you see the photo *who / that / where* I posted yesterday?

2 Is that the neighbour *who / which / where* made the cake for your birthday?

3 That building on the left is the office *which / who / where* I used to work.

4 The woman *where / who / which* usually cuts my hair has left.

5 He loves doing sports *where / that / who* he hasn't tried before.

6 She told me about a restaurant *that / where / which* they do really good vegetarian food.

7 We could meet at that French café – the one *which / where / who* you mentioned earlier.

8 For people *which / who / where* prefer peace and quiet, this hotel is perfect.

9 Is she the girl *that / where / which* you were telling me about?

10 This is the room *that / which / where* most of the meetings take place.

2 Combine the two sentences using a relative pronoun.

1 That's the hotel. We stayed there in May.

_____.

2 I've lost the necklace. Marta gave it to me for my birthday.

_____.

3 Did you hear the joke? Alan told it earlier.

_____.

4 She shouted to the boy. He had dropped his phone.

_____.

5 This is the bus. It goes to London.

_____.

6 Are they going to the club? It opened last month.

_____.

VOCABULARY: Relationships

3 Order the letters to make words that match the definitions.

1 someone who you share an apartment with TALFETAM _____

2 a person or organization that gives people work REPLOYME _____

3 someone who hates another person and tries to harm them MEENY _____

4 someone that you work with GLOECLEAU _____

5 someone that you live near to HENIGROUB _____

6 a man who is getting married or has just got married MOROG _____

7 someone that you own a company with SUBISSEN TRAPERN _____

8 the brother of your husband or wife, or your sister's husband ROBERTH-NI-WAL _____

4 Complete the words.

1 My father left when we were little, so my mother was a s___ ___ ___ ___ ___ parent.

2 My mother remarried and had a daughter, so I have a s___ ___ ___ ___ ___ ___ ___ ___ ___.

3 She has one cousin living near her, but no other r___ ___ ___ ___ ___ ___ ___ ___ .

4 I don't have brothers or sisters – I'm an o___ ___ ___ child.

5 Sarah doesn't get on with her husband's parents, but I love my parents-i___ -l___ ___.

6 My aunts and uncles all have children, so I have lots of c___ ___ ___ ___ ___ ___.

7 I didn't like the last guy I worked for, but my new b___ ___ ___ is great.

8 Enzo's g___ ___ ___ ___ ___ ___ ___ ___ ___ came to the club – they've been going out for six months.

PRONUNCIATION: Sentence stress

5 ▶12.1 Look at the relative pronouns *who*, *which* and *where*. Are they stressed (S) or unstressed (U)? Listen, check and repeat.

1 Who did you speak to? **S U**

2 That's the town where he grew up. **S U**

3 She must be the woman who works here. **S U**

4 Where are the instructions? **S U**

5 Did she say which train she was getting? **S U**

6 Which jacket looks better with these trousers? **S U**

SKILLS 12B

READING: Interpreting data

A

B

C

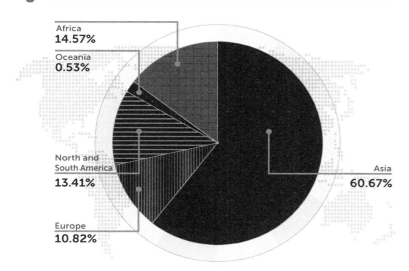

1 Match the information in figures A–C with three of 1–6.

1. World population by continent. ____
2. Average temperatures by continent. ____
3. Male and female life expectancy. ____
4. Average age of first marriage. ____
5. UK and US population change. ____
6. Life expectancy in the US and UK. ____

2 According to figures A–C, are these statements true (T) or false (F)?

1. Life expectancy in the USA rose by more than five years between 1990 and 2010. ____
2. In 1980, life expectancy for both UK and US citizens was still less than 75. ____
3. The difference between life expectancy in the UK and the USA increased between 1990 and 2010. ____
4. The average age difference between men and women for their first marriage is two years everywhere except Canada. ____
5. Chilean people are older at the time of their first marriage than other nationalities on this chart. ____
6. Brazilian women are the same age as women from the USA when they get married for the first time. ____
7. Asia has the highest population of any continent. ____
8. The population of Africa is about 3% larger than that of North and South America. ____
9. Fewer people live in North and South America than in Europe. ____

3 Choose the correct options to complete this summary of figure A.

> Figure A shows that from 1970 to 2012, UK citizens almost always lived slightly ¹*longer / shorter* lives than US citizens. Both groups have ²*increased / decreased* their life expectancy by ³*around / at least* 10 years during the period shown. Between 1970 and 1980, life expectancy for US citizens increased by ⁴*at least / nearly* five years. Between 1975 and 1995, figures for the UK and the USA were ⁵*not at all / roughly* similar. However, for a brief time around 1980, the life expectancy of US citizens was just ⁶*over / under* that of people in the UK. By 1982, life expectancy in both the US and the UK had reached ⁷*at least / almost* 75. By 2012, the average person in the UK could expect to live to ⁸*at least / nearly* 80.

69

12C LANGUAGE

GRAMMAR: Uses of the *-ing* form and the infinitive with *to*

1 Choose the correct options to complete the sentences.

1 I was disappointed ____ the exam.
   a to fail
   b failing

2 Before ____ , perhaps we should have something to eat.
   a to leave
   b leaving

3 She's just left the office ____ some lunch.
   a getting
   b to get

4 ____ is the best form of exercise.
   a To walk
   b Walking

5 I agree there's a problem, although I think it's unfair ____ Enzo.
   a blaming
   b to blame

6 It's not expensive ____ on a camping holiday.
   a going
   b to go

7 It was impossible not ____ her my secret!
   a to tell
   b telling

8 ____ time with friends is so important.
   a Spending
   b To spend

9 Not ____ meat can be difficult in some countries.
   a to eat
   b eating

2 Complete the sentences with the verbs in the box. Use each verb twice, once in the *-ing* form and once in the infinitive with *to*.

> earn   see   discuss   eat   speak

1 She was too afraid _____ to her boss about the situation.

2 We were both hungry, so we went home _____.

3 She's certainly keen on_____ a bit of cash.

4 After _____ the matter, we came to a decision.

5 Are you interested in _____ a film this evening?

6 _____ to a room of two hundred people is terrifying.

7 I'd be interested _____ her face when she hears the news!

8 I was delighted _____ a little extra money.

9 Bernando and I met _____ the problem.

10 _____ a lot of sugar is bad for your health.

VOCABULARY: Relationship verbs

3 Choose the correct options to complete the sentences.

1 I met a really nice girl on Saturday and thought I might ____ her **out**.
   a keep
   b ask
   c go

2 Yasmin and Javier ended their relationship but ____ **back together** last month.
   a got
   b fell
   c broke

3 Did you know that Ismail and Azra are ____ **married** next year?
   a making
   b getting
   c going

4 Yusuf and Elin used to go ____ **together**, but they split up.
   a on
   b in
   c out

5 Azra is **going on** a ____ tonight with a guy she met at work.
   a date
   b marriage
   c break

6 I've known Pablo for ten years. We ____ **friends** when we lived in London.
   a became
   b got
   c went

4 Complete the sentences.

1 Although Laura and I are from different countries, we manage to keep in _____.

2 They met and _____ in love while they were studying.

3 We have similar interests and opinions. Generally, we _____ a lot in common.

4 Nerea is single again. She broke _____ with her boyfriend a week ago.

5 Alejandro seems interesting. I'd like to _____ to know him better.

6 Isabella's great! I've always got _____ really well with her.

PRONUNCIATION: Word stress

5 ▶ 12.2 Match 1–8 with stress patterns a–e. Listen, check and repeat.

1 important ____
2 colleague ____
3 impossible ____
4 except ____
5 technology ____
6 better ____
7 afraid ____
8 probably ____

a O o
b o O
c o O o
d O o o
e o O o o

70

SKILLS 12D

SPEAKING: Giving thanks

1 ▶12.3 Listen to the conversation between Anna and Tim. Which four of these phrases do they use? Number them 1–4 in the order that you hear them.

a Thanks a lot. _____
b That's very kind of you. _____
c Thanks a million. _____
d Thanks. _____
e Thank you so much. _____
f Thanks very much. _____
g I can't thank you enough. _____
h I really appreciate it. _____
i I'm very grateful to you. _____

2 Read the four phrases from the conversation. Match them to the different ways of responding modestly.

1 Oh, I'm glad you like it. It's a really easy recipe. _____ _____
2 Not at all – it would be great fun. _____
3 It's nothing, really! _____
4 Well, not many other people entered, to be honest. _____

  a saying you are pleased
  b saying something isn't difficult
  c saying something is not as good as the other person thinks
  d saying you would enjoy doing something
  e saying something is only a small thing

3 ▶12.4 Listen to five people speaking. Choose the most appropriate response.

1 That's very kind of you. / Thanks.
2 Thanks a lot. / I'm very grateful to you.
3 Thanks very much. / I really appreciate it.
4 Thanks a lot. / I can't thank you enough.
5 I can't thank you enough. / Thanks a million.

4 ▶12.5 Listen to four people thanking, congratulating or complimenting you. Use your own ideas to respond modestly.

1 You're welcome. _____.
2 I'm glad you think so, but _____.
3 No problem. _____
4 Thanks. _____

5 ▶12.6 Listen to some possible answers to exercise 4.

71

12 REVIEW and PRACTICE

HOME   BLOG   **PODCASTS**   ABOUT   CONTACT

Tom and Sam talk about friendship and romance.

LISTENING

1 ▶ 12.7 Listen to the podcast. Are the statements true (T) or false (F), according to the speaker?

1 Sophie didn't get on with Marco to begin with. ___
2 Friendships can become romantic relationships. ___
3 What makes a good friend also makes a good partner. ___

2 ▶ 12.7 Listen again. Choose the correct options to complete the sentences.

1 Sophie met Marco at
 a school.
 b university.
 c work.
2 When they were at university, they
 a rarely spoke to each other.
 b never spoke to each other.
 c were in contact with each other.
3 In London, Sophie and Marco fell in love
 a over a period of time.
 b immediately.
 c with other people.
4 Sophie says that when two people start going out together, they
 a can be too honest with each other.
 b usually feel better about themselves.
 c often try to appear better than they are.
5 When Sophie started going out with Marco, she
 a already knew his personality.
 b didn't really like it.
 c found out new things about him.
6 Sophie says that people often choose a partner because
 a they have lots in common.
 b of their appearance.
 c of their honesty.
7 She says that finding someone physically attractive
 a may not be enough in a relationship.
 b is often bad for a relationship.
 c is usually good for a relationship.

READING

1 Read the blog about five people's problems. Complete 1–5 with the words in the box. There are three extra words.

> classmate   partners   boss   flatmate
> neighbours   colleagues   relative   girlfriend

2 Match the advice in 1–8 with problems A–E.

1 You should try to get to know the people you work with. ___
2 It's not a good idea to communicate with this person. ___
3 You might meet someone special through your friends. ___
4 You have to remember that most people are busy. ___
5 There's not much you can do to change this situation. ___
6 You need to think of conversations to have with these people. ___
7 Most people experience this at some point in their life. ___
8 You're unlikely to make friends at work. ___

72

REVIEW and PRACTICE 12

HOME BLOG PODCASTS ABOUT CONTACT

Tom and Sam give some advice about readers' problems.

You have your say

We've learnt so much about other people through writing this blog. Since this is our last one, we've invited our readers to write in with their problems to see if we can give them some advice.

A *We've just moved to a new town. No one speaks to us or shows any interest and we feel we're not welcome. Can you help?*

It's not that your ¹_____ dislike you – they're just getting on with their lives, going to work, seeing their friends, etc. and that doesn't leave much time for you! Why not invent a reason to speak to them? Ask when the next rubbish collection is, or which items you can recycle. People generally like to be helpful and the conversation might lead to other things.

B *I have a small company and my employees get on well. The problem is that they treat me differently. They never chat to me in their breaks or ask me out.*

To be honest, you probably just have to accept it. Your employees may respect you, even like you, but you're not their friend – you're their ²_____ and you have a different relationship with them. If you're short of friends, you need to look in other places.

C *I've just split up with my ³_____ and it's all I think about. I'm OK at work, but at home I don't know what to do with myself. I feel so sad and lonely.*

You probably won't like this, but you have to stop contacting her. The relationship's over – she's made that clear. Keeping in touch will make it worse. Get out and meet new people and you'll stop thinking about her.

D *I'm a single parent. I have great friends, but they're all getting married or have girlfriends or boyfriends and I'm always the lonely guy at the party. Any ideas?*

So your friends all have ⁴_____. It happens to everyone after a certain age. But why aren't they introducing you to their single friends? Why not suggest it? After all, if you get on with them, there's a good chance you'll get on with their friends. One of them may be your future partner!

E *I moved here recently for a new job and I don't know anyone. I'm single and I'm spending all my time alone. I'd love to make friends but I'm shy.*

Come on, don't wait for people to come to you! What about those new ⁵_____? Use your coffee breaks to get to know them. You'll soon find you have stuff in common and the next thing you know, you'll be watching films together!

73

WRITING PRACTICE

WRITING: Writing an essay

1 Read the essay about eating meat and put paragraphs A–E in order. Use the linkers to help you (*Firstly, The second reason, Finally, In conclusion*).

A ____ B ____ C ____ D ____ E ____

Should humans stop eating meat?

A The second reason is the environment. Raising animals for food produces gases that increase global warming. In addition, the animals need to be given huge amounts of water and grain. Also, some studies say that we would need twenty times less land to feed people instead of animals.

B People have been eating meat for thousands of years and they seem to love it. According to one report, the average American eats around 25 kilos of beef, 27 kilos of chicken and 22 kilos of pork in a year. But is it a good idea to go on like this? I don't believe that it is.

C In conclusion, I realize that many people love eating meat, but I would say that vegetarian food can be just as tasty. In any case, our world is changing. We are facing serious problems of climate change, obesity and disease, and in my view it's time for us to change too – before it's too late.

D Firstly, there's the question of the animals themselves. We go to a supermarket and buy a piece of meat in a package, but that meat was once a little lamb or a cute calf. Personally, I love all animals and I don't want to eat them!

E Finally, there is more and more evidence that eating fruit and vegetables is healthy and eating too much meat is not. I'm worried that diseases such as diabetes and heart disease are becoming more common because many people eat too much, and in particular too much meat.

2 The author talks about three main issues: protecting animals (A), the environment (E) and our health (H). Write the correct letter next to the arguments she uses.

1 There would be more food for people if we didn't eat meat. ____
2 A vegetarian diet is better than eating meat. ____
3 We don't think about animals enough when we eat them. ____
4 Eating meat may be increasing diseases. ____
5 The gas from keeping animals leads to global warming. ____
6 Obesity is a serious problem. ____

3 Read the opinions about 'meat-free Monday' – the idea that you should have one day a week without meat. Complete them with the words in the box, then say if each one is for (F) or against (A) meat-free Monday.

> believe   delighted   worried   say   bad   opinion   personally   good

1 In my _____, we need meat to stay strong and healthy.
2 _____, I feel much healthier when I don't eat meat.
3 It's always a _____ idea to eat more vegetables.
4 I _____ our bodies and teeth are designed to eat meat.
5 I'm _____ that farmers would suffer.
6 I would _____ that vegetarian food can be as tasty as meat.
7 I'm _____ that more people are giving up meat, because I love animals.
8 It's a _____ idea to stop eating meat, because it makes us stronger.

4 Write an essay on the subject 'Everyone should have a meat-free Monday'.

- You can use ideas from exercise 3 or your own ideas.
- Organize your ideas into five paragraphs: introduction, reasons 1–3, conclusion.
- Give examples and evidence to support your reasons.
- Use the linkers from exercise 1.

WRITING PRACTICE

WRITING: Writing a formal email

1 Read Ben's formal email complaining about his gym classes. What is the correct order of the paragraphs?

1 _____   2 _____   3 _____

To: info@gymsforall.co.uk

Subject: Exercise classes

[1]*Dear Sir/Madam*

A

In recent weeks, a large number of classes [2]*have been cancelled* without notice. [3]*In addition to this*, several of the teachers appear to be extremely inexperienced, leading to a real risk of injury.

B

In my opinion, all exercise instructors should [4]*be checked* regularly to [5]*ensure* that [6]*they are* teaching to the highest standards. Please would you let me know as soon as possible how you intend to make improvements to this unsatisfactory situation.

C

[7]*I am writing* [8]*with regard to* the standard of exercise classes at your gym, which I believe has reached an [9]*unacceptable* level.

[10]*Regards*,

Ben Southgate

2 Look at words and phrases 1–10 in the email and write the numbers next to the correct feature of formal emails.

Formal greeting	_____
Using full forms, not contractions	_____ _____
Formal words and expressions	_____ _____ _____ _____
Passives to avoid being personal	_____ _____
Formal ending	_____

3 Order the letters to form nouns to complete the sentences. What is the verb form of each noun?

1 The changing rooms need a lot of i_____.   NTPRMOEVME

2 Gym members need better instructions to avoid i_____.   RUJNY

3 Prices are already high. An i_____ is unreasonable.   RENCASE

4 Changes to class times have caused c_____.   NFUONOSI

5 The m_____ should run the gym more efficiently.   NTNAGAEME

6 We are not given enough i_____ about how to use the equipment safely.   NFROAMITNO

7 The d_____ that we were being given dirty towels was shocking.   COVISERY

8 I have made the d_____ to cancel my membership.   ISCENOI

9 Your plan to raise the price came as an unwelcome s_____.   REURPSI

4 You have received an email telling you that the cost of your gym membership is going up. You feel this is unreasonable because of the poor quality of the gym. Write a formal email of complaint.

- Include three paragraphs: say why you are writing, explain the situation, and say what you want to be done.
- Use the features of formal emails in exercise 2.
- Use the sentences in exercise 3 for ideas.

WRITING PRACTICE

WRITING: Making writing interesting

1 Read Eva's description of her first meeting with her neighbour. Choose the correct words to complete the text.

The first time I met Davina, I was quite <u>scared</u> of her! It was only the second day in my apartment when she knocked on my door to complain that I was being too <u>noisy</u>. ¹*However / As well / Although* it was two o'clock in the afternoon, she was wearing a pair of pyjamas with a huge old black coat over the top. Her long blonde hair was sticking up all over the place. She looked really <u>sleepy</u>, and really <u>angry</u>, ²*too / also / however*.

She told me she was a nurse and she was trying to sleep ³*because / so / that's why* she had been working all night. ⁴*But / That's why / And* she was wearing pyjamas. Of course, I apologized. I suddenly realized how <u>loud</u> my music was ⁵*because / too / so* I wasn't surprised she was <u>annoyed</u>.

I felt really bad. ⁶*Although / That's why / However*, the next day a card came through my door, inviting me for coffee at the weekend. That's when I discovered that Davina is really a lovely person when she's not <u>tired</u>!

Now we get on really well. We sometimes go out together, and I ⁷*also / as well / too* look after her friendly little brown and white cat when she goes away. Of course I'm not <u>frightened</u> of her any more, ⁸*but / because / also* I never play loud music now!

2 Look at the underlined words in Eva's description and make four pairs of synonyms.

3 Look at the adjectives in these sentences. Write them in the correct columns.

1 My flatmate is a **lovely young Italian** woman.
2 We sat at a **big round wooden** table.
3 Milo had **beautiful long brown** hair.
4 Hannah was wearing a **blue cotton** shirt.
5 Chris has a **fat old black** dog.
6 Karl cooks **delicious French** food.

opinion	size	shape	age	colour	nationality	material

4 Write about the first time you met someone you have a relationship with now, for example a neighbour, friend, colleague or flatmate.

- Use interesting adjectives, in the correct order, to describe things.
- Use synonyms to avoid repeating words.
- Use linkers to give reasons and results (*so, because, that's why*), to contrast information (*but, although, however*) or add information (*and, also, too, as well*).

NOTES

NOTES

NOTES

NOTES

NOTES

® Richmond

58 St Aldates
Oxford
OX1 1ST
United Kingdom

Printed in Brazil
ISBN: 978-84-668-2893-2
CP: 881148
DL: M-29778-2017
© Richmond / Santillana Global S.L. 2017

Printed in Brazil by Forma Certa Gráfica Digital
Lote: 777359
Cod: 290528932

All rights reserved. No part of this book may be reproduced, stored in a retrieval system or transmitted in any form by any means, electronic, mechanical, photocopying, recording or otherwise, without the prior permission in writing of the Publisher.

Publishing Director: Deborah Tricker
Publisher: Simone Foster
Media Publisher: Sue Ashcroft
Workbook Publisher: Luke Baxter
Content Developer: David Cole-Powney
Editors: Debra Emmett, Helen Ward, Ruth Cox, Emma Clarke, Fiona Hunt, Eleanor Clements, Helen Wendholt
Proofreaders: Peter Anderson, Amanda Leigh
Design Manager: Lorna Heaslip
Cover Design: This Ain't Rock'n'Roll, London
Design & Layout: Lorna Heaslip, Oliver Hutton
Photo Researcher: Magdalena Mayo
***Learning Curve* video:** Mannic Media
Audio production: Tom, Dick and Debbie, TEFL Audio
App development: The Distance

We would also like to thank the following people for their valuable contribution to writing and developing the material:
Alastair Lane, Bob McLarty, Claire Thacker, Louis Rogers, Rachael Roberts, Pamela Vittorio (Video Script Writer), Belen Fernandez (App Project Manager), Rob Sved (App Content Creator)

Illustrators:
Simon Clare; Dermot Flynn c/o Dutch Uncle; Guillaume Gennet, Julien Kern and Liav Zabari c/o Lemonade; Joanna Kerr c/o New Division; Piers Sandford c/o Meiklejohn; The Boy FitzHammond and Beverley Young, c/o NB Illustration

Photos:
J. Jaime; J. Lucas; 123RF/ lightpoet; ALAMY/IanDagnall Laptop Computing, John Birdsall, Chuck Place, Granger Historical Picture Archve, All Canada Photos, Cofiant Images, ONOKY - Photononstop, Action Plus Sports Images, Arcaid Images, Jasminko Ibrakovic, Image Source Salsa, Radius Images, Pat Behnke, Ann Cutting, 360b, Heritage Image Partnership Ltd, Roger Bamber, Cultura Creative (RF), Blend Images, RosaIreneBetancourt 10, Nick Gregory, BSIP SA, Trinity Mirror / Mirrorpix, Wavebreak Media ltd, Torontonian, Joy Sunny, SWNS, TP, IanDagnall Computing, PhotoEdit, Ammentorp Photography, Peter Barritt, Cliff Hide Stock, greenwales, caia image, eye35.pix, Carlos Guerra, Janine Wiedel Photolibrary, Peter Titmuss, Richard Heyes, Motoring Picture Library, Helen Hotson, Cephas Picture Library, ACORN 1, tommaso altamura, Steve Davey Photography, Image Source, Bill Cheyrou, Agencja Fotograficzna Caro, Kreative Photography, Imagedoc, Lou-Foto, Julie g Woodhouse, allesalltag, Stefano Carvoretto, MAX EAREY, wareham.nl (sport), Duncan Snow, Wilawan Khasawong, Brian Overcast, Design Pics Inc, Westend61 GmbH, Anton Stariskov, Elina Manninen, Aflo Co., Ltd., Alan Smith, Classic Image, Photos 12, D. Hurst, MBI, AF archive, PjrTravel, FineArt, moodboard, DonSmith, Jeramey Lende, epa european pressphoto agency b.v.; BNPS (BOURNEMOUTH NEWS & PICTURE SERVICE)/Rijksmuseum/ BNPS; CATERS NEWS AGENCY/ Caters News Agency;GETTY

IMAGES SALES SPAIN/Lumi Images/Dario Secen, Graham Monro/ gm photographics, Jetta Productions, Thomas_EyeDesign, Photos. com Plus, David M. Benett, Astrid Stawiarz, Mark Metcalfe, CARL DE SOUZA, Alistair Berg, Toby Burrows, Sam Edwards, Dave Hogan, Barcroft, Maskot, Bloomberg, Bettmann, Don Arnold, Kari Lehr, PETER MACDIARMID, RENE SLAMA, Boston Globe, CHRISTOPHE ARCHAMBAULT, Caiaimage/Paul Bradbury, Image source, Paul Chesley, Thinkstock; HIGHRES PRESS STOCK/AbleStock.com; ISTOCKPHOTO/SeanShot, Pali Rao, oztasbc, jojoo64, SondraP, MollyNZ, Geber86, xijian, vgajic, sturti, olaser, miralex, mergez, alexsl, HASLOO, SolStock, DONOT6, Getty Images Sales Spain, Devasahayam Chandra Dhas, monkeybusinessimages, Osmany Torres Martín, alessandroguerriero, AleksandarGeorgiev, Tommaso Altamura, Nicolas McComber, warrengoldswain, travellinglight, stevecoleimages, Robyn Mackenzie, German-skydiver, digitalskillet, Wavebreakmedia, Petar Chernaev, Jaroslav Frank, wundervisuals, Squaredpixels, LuckyBusiness, Julia Nichols, Drazen Lovric, Dean Mitchell, elenaleonova, PeopleImages, Elenathewise, Dieter Meyrl, Daniel Ernst, Cathy Yeulet, ozgurdonmaz, mediaphotos, Yuri_Arcurs, Visiofutura, Jason Poole, David Sucsy, Bulent Ince, nataistock, bluehill75, calvindexter, MartialRed, Juanmonino, FangXiaNuo, Joel Carillet, FSTOPLIGHT, DeluXe-PiX, DeanDrobot, g-stockstudio, zhudifeng, pixdeluxe, milanfoto, dolgachov, cindygoff, SteveTram, OcusFocus, robertcicchetti, Maxiphoto, Kaan Ates, Huchen Lu, Anna Bryukhanova, Halfpoint, CactuSoup, yipengge, mihailomilovanovic, urbancow, rcaucino, pepifoto, lucky336, kyoshino, denphumi; MAYANG MURNI ADNIN; NASA/ NASA; REX SHUTTERSTOCK/Jonathan Player, ABC Inc/Everett, Peter Brooker, Kippa Limited, Pixelformula, Newspix; SHUTTERSTOCK; SHUTTERSTOCK NETHERLANDS,B.V.; Project Jacquard/Levi's Strauss; Library of Congress/wikipedia; Carpigiani Gelato University; Niccolo Casas /EMBR labs; Optomen Television Ltd.; courtesy of Alex Deans; Pauline Van Dongen; Alastair Humphreys; freepic.com; Ringly Inc.; Jon Barlow; Dave Homcy; ALAMY/Frances Roberts, Nick Baylis, REUTERS, David Taylor, Paul Nichols, Mode Images, M L Pearson, Jeremey Richards, Panther Media GmBH, Big Cheese Photo LLC, Digital Image Library, Sabena Jane Blackbird, www. BibleLandPictures.com, Purcell Team; GETTY IMAGES SALES SPAIN/Thinkstock; ISTOCKPHOTO/Getty Images Sales Spain; REX SHUTTERSTOCK/Solent News; ARCHIVO SANTILLANA

Cover Photo: Jon Barlow

We would like to thank the following reviewers for their valuable feedback which has made Personal Best possible. We extend our thanks to the many teachers and students not mentioned here.
Brad Bawtinheimer, Manuel Hidalgo, Paulo Dantas, Diana Bermúdez, Laura Gutiérrez, Hardy Griffin, Angi Conti, Christopher Morabito, Hande Kokce, Jorge Lobato, Leonardo Mercato, Mercilinda Ortiz, Wendy López

The Publisher has made every effort to trace the owner of copyright material; however, the Publisher will correct any involuntary omission at the earliest opportunity.